T0368104

How Can You Be So Calm?

LEANING ON GOD THROUGH CANCER

BILL GREENWADE

WESTBOW
PRESS®
A DIVISION OF THOMAS NELSON
& ZONDERVAN

WestBow Press books may be ordered through booksellers or by contacting:

WestBow Press
A Division of Thomas Nelson & Zondervan
1663 Liberty Drive
Bloomington, IN 47403
www.westbowpress.com
844-714-3454

ISBN: 979-8-3850-4349-1 (sc)
ISBN: 979-8-3850-4350-7 (hc)
ISBN: 979-8-3850-4351-4 (e)

Library of Congress Control Number: 2025901937

Print information available on the last page.

WestBow Press rev. date: 02/06/2025

Forward

I first met Bill in 1984 when we worked together for the same company in Houston, TX. He's a proud Texan who was new to me as a Chicago transplant, and I immediately liked him. I enjoyed his company, his pleasant demeanor, common sense, and especially our shared interest in motorcycles. Even after I moved away in 1994, our friendship only strengthened. I've always believed time and distance apart are unimportant in a good relationship.

When Bill told me about his cancer diagnosis and possible bone marrow transplant, I was stunned. I know little about cancer treatments and nothing about bone marrow transplants. Only once had someone close to me been touched with cancer. Bill's situation instantly became powerfully real to me, and I prayed for him daily...I still do.

As our phone calls became more frequent, he explained the treatment decision he was facing, the need for identifying a "perfect" donor, and the probable outcomes. This news was all very sobering and scary for me. But Bill was still able to enjoy wonderful moments of levity. We joked about the possibility of the donor not being a Texan, possibly an "Okie"? A suitable donor was identified, which was a blessing, and the transplant was performed. Once his post-op treatments began, Bill posted detailed updates daily. I was struck by the incredibly dedicated and diligent medical attention he was receiving, and it was clear he was in the right place for the care he needed. I forwarded these daily updates to mutual friends, so everyone was kept informed. Bill and I had never discussed faith and God previously, but I noticed more frequent references to God that quickly became regular content. Clearly God was a part of Bill's life, and in a big way.

In the hospital, doctors demand patients be up and walking post-surgery as soon as possible which is the last thing you feel like doing. More levity: having spent months in the hospital myself after a motorcycle crash years ago and doing lots of walking, I suggested that when walking he made certain the opening in the back of his hospital gown was closed...for everyone's benefit. Bill's daily walks got longer and began to include talks about faith with fellow walkers, employees, and it seemed just about anyone he met. His attitude seemed to always be positive, his faith strong, and I looked forward to his updates because they were, and continue to be, inspiring. Even more levity: Bill walked so much that as a Scoutmaster I felt compelled to award him an honorary Hiking merit badge.

Extended recovery always includes ups and downs, progress and setbacks. But Bill's attitude remained positive because of the devoted support of his wife Debbi, a circle of loving friends and family, his church community, and his faith. We often talked about how God holds the hands of those who believe, and Bill's writing and conversations leave no doubt in our minds. And today, who would have guessed that Bill would begin studying to become a minister? His strong faith and his desire to share it and his story with others are very real!

Bill and I share several parallels in our lives. Prior to my motorcycle accident in 2005 I was what I describe as a lazy Christian. I grew up in a family that always went to church, celebrated Easter and Christmas, and gave me a strong foundation. However, when I went off to college with its many distractions, I turned away from God. For many years life was good...until I woke up in the ICU very broken, scared, and the most vulnerable and helpless I'd ever felt in my life. My prayer was to ask God what he wanted me to do with my life, and my commitment was to follow Him. God's answer was not a road to Damascus experience, which as an engineer I would have preferred, but rather a more subtle response that has cemented my faith and led to a life of service to others. I thank God daily for the new perspectives that accident brought to my life.

When Bill heard of my accident, without hesitation he came to see me, be with me, and pray for me. His being there was a great comfort to my family, especially since I was in a coma. It's a special privilege to have this man as my friend, one who will always have my back, and I in turn, his. I cherish Bill's friendship and admire how he has dealt with his medical challenges. His faith, and his desire to share his story with others, is an inspiration for all.

Steve Wenger

Introduction

When I was born, my father was 25 and my mother was 19. I was the oldest of five children. My father worked six days a week as the butcher in a grocery store, and my mother stayed home, taking care of our home and raising us kids. We moved a lot when I was young. I was born in McAllen, TX near the southern tip of the state. I went to first grade in Lawton, Oklahoma and started second grade back in South Texas. We moved to Refugio, Texas near the Gulf Coast mid-way through my second-grade year, and I graduated from High School there. I remember having a Lone Ranger metal lunchbox in first grade and starting each morning in second grade reciting the Pledge of Allegiance and The Lord's Prayer. An ice cream truck would pull onto the playground at recess, and we could buy treats.

Our family would travel to visit my grandparents and other relatives often, and we would go to my uncle's farm near Waco, Texas every year to visit several days. I have fond memories of large family gatherings for reunions and holidays. We lived in the country, several miles from town. We had horses, a milk cow, chickens, pigs, and dogs. My father loved horses and cattle, and he and I would often work on nearby ranches on his days off from his regular job.

I had good parents. I don't remember ever hearing them have an argument. They loved each other too much to argue, I suppose. And they loved us kids. I never heard any profanity from my parents. It just wasn't in their vocabulary, I guess. My parents never drank alcohol. Daddy was severely diabetic, and alcohol was never in our house. He did smoke cigarettes, though. So did my grandparents.

My parents didn't talk about God or faith. We didn't go to church as a family, except occasionally on Easter. I went to Sunday school, but I couldn't tell you how often or for how long. I found out after my mother died that she would take us to town and drop us off at the church for Sunday school and come back and pick us up afterwards. We were raised in a home that abided by the Ten Commandments, although I don't remember either of my parents referencing scripture. I do remember my grandmother citing scripture. I remember her saying "God will never give you a burden you can't handle". She gave me my first Bible when I was six years old, and I still have it. As a child, I believed in God and knew Jesus had died for our sins and was resurrected, but I wasn't baptized until many years later.

Daddy died when I was 14. I was helping him at the grocery store, he went into diabetic shock, and we went immediately to the Emergency Room at our local hospital. My mother came to the hospital, and he died of a heart attack within an hour. I drove his pickup truck home. Relatives came for his funeral, neighbors helped my mother file for his Social Security and Veteran benefits, and she went to work at the bank in town. We couldn't sell his pickup because he died without a will. I drove it to school and back and worked part-time jobs after school and summers.

I graduated from Refugio High School and was accepted at Texas A&M University, where I was in the Corps of Cadets my freshman year. I worked as a waiter in the dining hall and later as a student machinist to pay my way through college. I graduated in 1975. I only occasionally went to church in High School and College. I was concentrating on making good grades so I wouldn't have to go to Viet Nam.

During the next 40 years, I married, had children, climbed career ladders, divorced, married again, divorced again and went to church off and on. I was baptized in 1990 when I was 37 years old. My faith was hot and cold. I would get involved in church for a while, and then I would stop going. I was asked to be a deacon in one of the churches I attended, and then the offer was taken back when they found I'd been divorced. I read my Bible, attended churches, and watched sermons online without any consistency. I had ups and downs in those 40 years, dreams came true, and dreams were shattered. Money was made and lost. Marriages failed. I always rebounded and recovered. I never got mad at God. I never blamed Him for my failures. I rarely gave Him credit for my successes. I had too much faith in me.

By the year 2020, I thought I was living the dream. Nearly everything I owned was in my Winnebago motorhome and the cargo trailer I pulled behind it. For the past several years, I had traveled around the United States, volunteering at National Parks and State Parks and private RV campgrounds in some of the most beautiful locations in this country. I also worked part-time doing risk assessments of ranches and farms in areas wherever I traveled. I would go north to cooler temperatures in the summer and come back to Texas to warmer temperatures in the winter and spend Thanksgiving and Christmas holidays with family. On every trip I made sure to go through Granbury, Texas to visit with my uncle Bill. Life was good.

In March of 2020, I was on my way from Texas to California to volunteer at an RV campground among the giant redwoods. I got a call from Beverly, a close friend in Granbury, asking if I was able to come to my uncle Bill's assistance. He had fallen and broken his ankle, had surgery, and was wearing a "boot" that allowed him to walk while it healed. While wearing the boot, he tripped when it caught on the rug in his closet, he fell and fractured his hip, had surgery again, and was transferred to a rehab facility. At that time, many precautions and restrictions for the COVID pandemic were in place, and therefore my uncle could not have visitors. He wanted to go home and wanted me to come help him until he could get back on his feet. I gladly said yes, made a U-turn as soon as possible, and headed to Granbury. Beverly and two other very close friends of my uncle, J.L. and Judy, met me in Granbury and we moved my uncle Bill from the rehab facility to his home. I parked my motorhome in a nearby storage facility and my dog Hope and I moved in temporarily with him.

Beverly lived just three houses down the street from my uncle, in the small neighborhood of Fountain Village. She was a close friend of my uncle and a Registered Nurse. Beverly would walk over and visit and was instrumental in his care. I mostly followed her advice and directions, and we shared time caring for him, which allowed me to leave the house for errands and to walk my dog, Hope. On one of our first walks, Hope and I met Becky, who was working in her flower bed. We introduced ourselves and I explained why I was there, and that she would likely see me walking Hope often. On subsequent walks, we met other Fountain Village neighbors and explained who we were and why we were there. Each time I met a new neighbor, I would tell my Uncle Bill and Beverly who I had met. One day Hope and I met Debbi and her granddaughter Jade, who were walking Debbi's new puppy Bella. The dogs were naturally curious about each other and sniffed each other from head to tail. Debbi introduced herself and Jade, who was visiting for a few days. She asked who I was and was I a new homeowner or was I visiting someone in the neighborhood. I pointed to my Uncle Bill's home just across the street from where we were standing and explained how I got there. She pointed to her home eight houses down the street and said she'd lived in Fountain Village for six years.

When I returned and told my Uncle Bill and Beverly that I'd met Debbi and Jade, you would have thought I'd met the Pope outside. It turned out they were both secretly matchmaking and couldn't wait for Debbi and me to meet each other. Debbi and my Uncle Bill had been members of a Bible Study group, and my Uncle Bill was especially fond of Jade, who he doted over every time she visited. Debbi and I began walking our dogs together often, each time sharing more information about ourselves – past and present. We were immediate friends, and soon realized our first meeting was the fairy tale "love at first sight". We believe our meeting was a God moment.

For months my Uncle Bill was in and out of emergency rooms and hospitals due to complications related to his surgeries and his unwillingness to cooperate with physical therapists and follow doctors' orders. It was so frustrating to try and help him get better and have him resist helping himself. He would say "I'll be OK, I'll just rest in my recliner and the rest will get me better." He didn't get better. He would not eat or drink properly, would end up dehydrated and with electrolyte imbalances and was in and out of the hospital until they could stabilize and release him to go back home.

Debbi and I spent more time together and I proposed to her on the corner where we had originally met. We started thinking about a wedding date, which was extremely difficult considering the travel restrictions and health precautions in place due to COVID. We were married on August 29, 2020 in a beautiful little chapel just a few miles from her neighborhood, and we had a lovely wedding in spite of a small crowd and most wearing masks as precautions. It was a special day for Debbi and me and always will be.

My uncle refused to attend our wedding because he didn't want to be a "spectacle" in a wheelchair, which was heartbreaking. I believe pride was what kept him away. He had been a strong, successful man. He didn't want to be seen weak. He continued not exercising, not eating and not drinking properly. I believe pride was again a big factor. He passed away during one of the hospitalizations in September. Watching him die that way made me realize how self-destructive it is to rely on what others think of us. My mother and youngest brother refused to attend our wedding due to COVID fears, again heartbreaking.

In the next two years, Hope and I moved into Debbi's home, we went to Stonewater Church together, and I continued to do risk assessment work part-time. We discovered I had cancer, found there were only three specialists in the United States who were experts in the type of cancer I had, one just 60 miles away, in Dallas. I could have been in Montana, Florida, or any other remote location over a thousand miles away. But there I was, called to help my uncle, now living less than 100 miles from the best doctor for my rare cancer, married to a loving wife willing to support me, member of a loving church family, and very close to several of my other family members. It is amazing how God puts pieces of our lives together and we don't even know what He's doing until it is blatantly obvious. This was not coincidence. His timing is perfect.

This is my story of joy in suffering. How leaning on God through my cancer treatment and recovery gave me peace beyond understanding. How God used my suffering to strengthen me and sharpen my faith and draw me closer to Him. There have been opportunities and rewards I never anticipated. If you are currently battling cancer or any other life-threatening disease, my hope is that you will relate to some of my experiences and lean on your faith. If you are questioning your faith, I hope you will accept Jesus as your Savior, place your trust in Him and become a believer in the miracle of God's grace.

> "Fear not, for I am with you; be not dismayed, for I am your God, I will strengthen you, Yes I will help you, I will uphold you with My righteous right hand." Isaiah 41:10, NKJV

"You Have Cancer"

Early symptoms

In June 2020, my primary care physician was reviewing the lab work from my routine annual physical and said, "Your labs look great, except for the high platelet count". She noted that the level had increased since my last visit and recommended a follow up visit in six months to see if the platelet count continued to rise. In December, my platelet count was even higher. My doctor recommended more extensive lab work and ordered a pathologist smear in two weeks to assess if a reactive process was happening, because she was concerned about a "possible bone marrow malignancy." Late December results from the pathologist smear showed normal red blood cell population, without anemia and no significant abnormalities. I had a routine physical in June 2021 and my lab results showed my platelet count was lower, but still out of the "normal" range. My doctor was not concerned because the count was only slightly above the normal range. Another "flag" in my lab analysis was the RDW, which is related to red blood cell size and distribution, and it was only slightly out of the normal range again, so my doctor was not concerned. At my next physical in October 2021, the same two "flags" appeared – my platelet count was lower than the last reading but still out of the normal range, and my RDW had increased. Neither of these concerned my doctor, who recommended we continue to monitor annually.

By June of 2022, fatigue was starting to bother me. I was still doing normal activities, but it was noticeable (and frustrating) how quickly and often I would get tired. Blood work resulted in several flags this time. My platelet count went from 439 to 233, now within the normal range, but I wanted to know why it would take such a nosedive after being high for over two years? The other flags included RBC (red blood cell count), which was on the low side of normal, Hemoglobin (protein in red blood cells) out of the normal range, and Hematocrit (the percentage of red blood cells in the blood) also low and out of the normal range. When I asked my doctor about these flags, she didn't seem concerned, and said it was common to have similar readings associated with being slightly anemic, which often results in fatigue. She ordered an iron panel to determine if I was anemic due to low iron level, AND to maybe satisfy my displeasure with what I thought were significant changes in my lab test results. Results of the iron panel were completely normal, so we knew my anemia had nothing to do with iron level.

My doctor recommended we repeat the lab work again in 60 days, so in August 2022 we got lab results back that showed five flags this time. RBC, hemoglobin, and hematocrit continued to decrease, and though my platelet count was still within the normal range, it had gone down by another 20%. My doctor ordered another pathology review, and the findings were normal, so she recommended we continue to monitor every 60 days.

By this time, I was really getting anxious about no definitive answers. We had done blood work and pathology reviews several times. There wasn't much promise in doing the same thing over and over and expecting different results (the clinical definition of insanity). Maybe I should have tried to get a second opinion, but Medicare wouldn't pay just because I was unhappy with some test results. They needed to see an understandable reason for re-testing.

Here I'd like to emphasize being your own strongest advocate. If you have a question about your medical condition or test results, talk to your doctor and ask questions to be sure you understand what's going on. Ask them to slow down with their explanations and talk in terms you can understand and take notes. Some doctors may even let you record your conversations. I found that most of the time they are pleased you are interested.

My exhaustion continued. We bought a new bed because I wasn't sleeping well, thinking maybe lack of sleep was contributing to my lack of energy. Other than being tired more often, my life was normal and busy. I continued doing my part-time consulting work and even went on a whirlwind trip from Texas to Utah, Idaho and Wyoming, completing over a dozen risk assessments and driving over 4,000 miles in two weeks.

On September 24, 2022, I was walking our dogs in our neighborhood and began to feel a sharp pain in my upper back every time I took a breath. The pain was severe enough to not ignore, and I asked my wife Debbi to take me to the local hospital emergency room. I was tested for a heart attack (negative), a stroke (negative) and then had a CT scan, which revealed I had a saddle pulmonary embolism (PE), which is a blood clot that becomes lodged where the main pulmonary artery divides and branches to the right and left lungs.

I was told "This is very serious – a saddle pulmonary embolism can kill you", given a double dose of blood thinner, released, and told to make an appointment with a hematologist ASAP. Saddle PEs are very rare, accounting for only 2% of all PEs. We read that studies have shown 25% of people who develop a saddle PE die instantly, and another 30% die within 3 months. Good grief! I had one of those "life flashes before your eyes" moments. When I was a kid, a rattlesnake struck at me, and I jumped back just enough that it missed. I was hit broadside by a Buick while riding my motorcycle and walked away from the accident. I fell asleep driving in college and totaled my vehicle, again walking away and receiving only a few stitches. I felt like I had again just been missed by a runaway truck!

The next day we called to make an appointment with my primary care physician because we knew it was required before I could be referred to a specialist. Three days later, when we got to her office, we were told we would meet with one of her staff, a P.A. (Physician's Assistant). He looked at the emergency room records and listened to our account of events and repeated "This is very serious – a saddle pulmonary embolism can kill you". We told him we would like to be referred to a hematologist in Granbury who Debbi was familiar with. The P.A. said OK, but then added "if he can't see you right away, give me a call and I know somebody I can contact who will." Although I was nervous about having the pulmonary embolism, I really didn't have any serious symptoms – no pain, no trouble breathing, and no difficulty doing normal things like walking the dogs or driving.

We called the hematologist's office and was told he was on vacation and the soonest we could get an appointment was October 12. We couldn't believe it! Two different doctors had just told us "This can kill you – get to a specialist right away." We called the P.A. as he had recommended and were told by the office nurse to leave a message, and he would call us back. Now we were really getting frustrated.

When the P.A. called us back, he referred us to a hematologist in the same hospital system as my primary care doctor and we called right away to make an appointment. We were politely told the soonest we could get an appointment would be some time in November. We decided to stick with the October appointment with the hematologist in Granbury.

Tension was high at our house. Frustration was high. We were upset because we had been told repeatedly how serious and dangerous my condition was, then told to wait. But the silver lining was that I was not in the morgue where 25% of people go immediately, I was not in I.C.U. where most people are admitted immediately, I was not even in a hospital, and I was not in any pain.

Debbi was so frustrated because we heard several medical professionals say the same thing – "This can be fatal, so you need to see a specialist immediately", and she felt helpless. Debbi had lost her two previous husbands to cancer. She later told me she would put her hand on my chest several times every night when I was sleeping to be sure I was still breathing.

TESTS

On October 12, we met with the hematologist in Granbury to get to the bottom of what caused my pulmonary embolism and what to do about it. When we parked in front of the building that had big letters on the side that said ONCOLOGY, it was not a good feeling. "Oncology is cancer", I remember thinking to myself, and "I have a clot, not cancer".

The doctor was polite and professional, but almost to a fault. He only briefly explained what the embolism was and told me to get on the internet and do some research for more details. He echoed "This is serious and can kill you" and said I would likely be taking blood thinners the rest of my life to prevent future clots. He wanted to look at the results of the blood work from the emergency room, and ordered more blood taken to be analyzed by their own lab. He asked several questions about my medical history, had I ever had clots of any sort in my legs, was I active or sedentary, etc. but he didn't speculate as to what exactly caused the embolism. We made an appointment for a follow up visit in a week to discuss the lab results.

Two days later, I was again walking our dogs around the neighborhood when suddenly I had chest pains like somebody was pushing against my upper chest, and both my hands went numb with that pins and needles feeling. I was very close to our house, but I couldn't open the front door when I got home because my hands were numb. We loaded up and went straight to the E.R. again. When we arrived, I was put in a room right away, my vitals were checked, a nitroglycerin pill was put under my tongue, and an I.V. was placed to draw blood for lab analysis.

The numbness in my hands went away quickly, and the pain in my chest soon subsided. The attending doctor asked me several questions and I was soon wheeled into X-Ray. The lab work showed there were no enzymes that indicated I'd had a heart attack, and the doctor concluded I'd had an episode of angina, probably because of increased strain on my heart from the pulmonary embolism. His advice: get to my cardiologist ASAP. That same day (the E.R. visit was near midnight) we were able to have a tele-visit with my cardiologist and we scheduled tests for later that month.

Our wall calendar was now becoming dominated by doctor appointments. On October 19 we met again with the hematologist to go over their lab results, and he said he saw evidence of some "funky" cells in my blood. He confirmed that the heart episode was likely from increased stress caused by the embolism but deferred to my cardiologist. He explained that all blood cells are made in the bone marrow, and we needed to look in the "factory" to get a better idea of where the funky blood cells were coming from and a possible cause of the pulmonary embolism. He scheduled a bone marrow biopsy for the following week. On October 21, we had an in-person visit with my cardiologist, who ordered and scheduled an EKG and echocardiogram.

On October 25, my bone marrow biopsy was done. I had heard a variety of accounts from friends and family about painful and not-so-painful biopsies they had experienced, and I was anxious about it. I woke up the night before from having dreams about the procedure. The staff were very understanding and did a great job of explaining exactly how it would be done. I had very little pain during and after the procedure. Note to self: read Matthew 6:34 again, about not worrying about tomorrow. It does nothing but waste energy to worry about something that hasn't happened yet. It probably won't happen the same way you worried it would. In a couple of weeks, we would meet again with the doctor to discuss the results.

On October 30, the EKG and echocardiogram were done at my cardiologist's office. On November 2, I had another C.T. scan done. On November 4, we met with my cardiologist, who was happy to report my EKG and echocardiogram results were normal. No heart issues. Praise God! See what I mean about our calendar being filled up with doctor appointments?

Anybody who has medical appointments these days knows about patient portals; those computer recordkeeping apps that now store all your medical records and make them available to you via your computer or even your cell phone. I get emails and texts from my patient portals reminding me of upcoming appointments, telling me of after-visit summaries, and continuously asking me to complete customer satisfaction surveys. These portals are a blessing and a curse. You can see results of tests on your portals and not have to wait to see your doctor at a follow up visit. But they can be a curse because you get results, but you don't completely understand them, or you are not sure you're interpreting them properly, then you can't talk to your doctor for weeks!

One of the emails notified me that I had new test results available on one of my patient portals. I logged on, found the latest records and read the summary of my last CT scan: "No evidence of pulmonary embolism." How could that be? Was I reading this wrong? Had someone made a mistake? We were so excited to read this, and thanked God! We couldn't wait to talk to the doctor about it to see if it was accurate. We had to resist announcing it to our friends and family until we got the doctor's confirmation.

DIAGNOSIS

We met again with the hematologist to review the results of the bone marrow biopsy, and we got good news and bad news. The good news was his confirmation that the pulmonary embolism had completely resolved itself, with no remaining evidence! He didn't speculate how it disappeared so quickly, just reiterated that it was important I keep taking the blood thinner for future clot prevention. I believe God was saying "OK, I have your attention now, so no need for this embolism any longer." The not-so-good news – the doctor explained that I had a very rare bone marrow cancer called Primary Myelofibrosis with the JAK2 mutation. Again, he said we should do our own research, noted that it is not normally an aggressive cancer, but it could not be treated with chemotherapy or radiation. He added that there are no medications to prevent it or slow it down. The only "cure" was a bone marrow transplant. He explained that it would be a high-risk option due to my age and several other factors. He recommended we make an appointment with a bone marrow transplant specialist who would explain the procedure and the risks involved and if a transplant was something we should do now or consider later. He recommended I come to the clinic every 90 days for blood analysis to monitor the cancer's progression. He added that the prognosis could be living with myelofibrosis for several years or perhaps only a couple. He was now my oncologist.

PEACE

I don't know about you, but I had seen friends and family die from cancer, and wondered how I would react if I was given news that I had a terminal illness. Would I be mad? Would I be frightened? We've all seen movies and TV shows trying to depict such a situation. The moment the doctor told us I had cancer it was like time stopped. I felt as if I was sitting under a waterfall, but instead of water, I felt covered with peace, and one of my favorite scriptures came to mind:

> "Therefore, do not worry about tomorrow, for tomorrow
> will worry about its own things. Sufficient for the day is
> its own trouble." Matthew 6:34, NKJV

This feeling of peace remained with me throughout my entire cancer experience. Debbi did not have the same reaction. Having lost two previous husbands to brain cancer and kidney cancer, she was not at peace with this news. She wanted to do something about it. She didn't understand why God would bring us together and then give me cancer after she had already lost two husbands she loved to cancer!

The doctor went on to explain that Primary Myelofibrosis (MF) is a rare, chronic blood cancer called a myeloproliferative neoplasm (MPN) where scar tissue forms in the bone marrow and impairs its ability to produce normal blood cells. Bone marrow is where blood cells are made. In MF, the bone marrow produces abnormal cells due to a change (or mutation) in the DNA. As the cells divide, they pass along the mutation to the new cells. Eventually, abnormal cells crowd out normal, healthy cells and disrupt the production of red and white blood cells and platelets. An analogy the doctor used was to imagine my bone marrow as a hallway, with the MF likened to spiders building webs across the hallway. Eventually, the spider webs become so numerous that you can no longer walk through the hallway. MF builds scar tissue in the bone marrow that eventually blocks pathways for new blood cells produced by your bone marrow and chokes off your immune system. He added that there were no chemotherapy or radiation treatments available. MF is chronic, meaning that it lasts for a long period of time and may never go away. It also has the potential to "progress" or get worse over time. We made an appointment to meet with the transplant doctor on November 28. In the meantime, we did some research and found out that there were only three MPN specialists in the United States who had experience with myelofibrosis transplants. One of them was the doctor we had an appointment with.

Most of my life, I thought I could fix about anything. It was only a few years ago that I realized I hadn't fixed past marriages, I hadn't fixed job conflicts, and I hadn't fixed a lot of things because I just figured I would move on, start over, and recover. I did move on and start over, but I left a lot of collateral damage behind. In this case, I felt helpless. I didn't know a thing about fixing cancer. I felt like I needed to learn how to fix cancer. I needed to comfort Debbi. I needed to prepare for a fight. I needed to notify friends and family. I felt overwhelmed. I didn't know what to do first. I prayed and prayed, and I gave it to God and asked Him to tell me what He wanted me to know and what He wanted me to do. I remembered the scripture

> "Trust in the Lord with all your heart, And lean not on your own understanding; In all your ways acknowledge Him, And He shall direct your paths." Proverbs 3:5-6, NKJV

Watch and Wait

At this point, we entered the stage of watching my symptoms and changes in my blood test results and waiting to see how long it might be until I needed a transplant. Then we would wait on a donor to be found.

I let our immediate families know what was going on. It wasn't long before they started telling other family and friends and I soon began getting emails and texts wanting more information. There was an outpouring of concern and notices that I was in everyone's prayers, which meant a lot to me and Debbi. I sent emails to relatives and close friends to share as many details as we could. Debbi volunteered in Help Ministry at our church, and she told co-workers. At the next Sunday morning service we attended, several members asked how I was doing and said they were praying for us.

I sent updates every time I would have another doctor appointment or had to go to the lab for more blood work and kept everyone up to date right up to when we got the news about the cancer and the oncologist's plan to do blood work every 90 days to monitor the cancer's progress. There was nothing more to communicate except thank-you for the friendships, love, and prayers and that I would let everybody know more as soon as WE knew more.

On November 28, we had an appointment with the transplant doctor in Dallas. He is a myeloproliferative neoplasm (MPN) specialist and the reason for our visit was to learn what the bone marrow transplant involves, how they determine the right time to do one, the risks, and how the donor search works. There were some major takeaways from this consultation. It is very easy to assume that a bone marrow transplant is a major, complicated procedure. They are done very often. Hospitals have done thousands over the years. While that is true, we learned that the decision to have a bone marrow transplant is often not routine. It is a difficult choice that must be made based on many risk factors. The doctor explained that age and physical condition are paramount. There are several risks involved in the pre-op stage, where radiation and/or chemotherapy drugs are used to "kill" all the existing cells in the bone marrow to ensure the mutated cells are gone before the new stem cells are transplanted. When you no longer have essential blood cells, there is a high risk of infection from any number of sources. Then there are the risks during the procedure, from anesthesia if necessary and other sources. There is the post-transplant period when there is a risk that the transplanted bone marrow will reject your body as its new home and may begin attacking different organs in the body. This is known as GVHD, or Graft vs. Host Disease. Another thing we learned is that there are huge networks of bone marrow donors…30 million donors in the BeTheMatch database at the time. And we would probably not need a family member donor because a match was normally relatively easy to find. The key was getting as close a match as possible to avoid GVHD rejection.

I stress here how important it is to listen to your doctors and ask as many questions as they are willing to answer. They have done the procedures. The have seen the successes and the failures. They know the risks involved. Our main takeaway from the meeting was that a bone marrow transplant is really a "last resort", and you must weigh risk vs. benefits. We were very grateful for the doctor's time and honesty.

Not a day went by that I didn't think about the cancer. Every morning, I would fix coffee and step out to the patio and thank God for another new day. Debbi's co-workers and other staff at Stonewater Church would always ask her "how is Bill?" or "how is that husband of yours?" and my name was written on the prayer board in the staff offices hallway. Every Sunday greeters and ushers at church would meet us with hugs and handshakes and want to know how I was feeling. There was such a network of friends and church members praying for us – and we were so grateful.

Without any serious symptoms, it was easy to have normal days, but occasionally Debbi and I were both overcome by emotions. We would fall into that trap of worrying about tomorrow – her being afraid of living without me, and me being afraid of dying and not being able to care for Debbi. I thought of ridiculous details like who would help walk the dogs every day, check the car tires, fix things around the house and help find her iPhone when she misplaced it. The unknown can be frightening. I relied on the knowledge that we have a loving God, and scripture says to not worry about tomorrow. We would hug and talk about our fears sometimes, but many tears were shed separately and in private. We often reminded each other that we could be killed in a car accident more suddenly than the cancer, and we didn't worry every day about a car accident. We remembered that God gives us one good day after another, and He could take the cancer away in an instant if it was His will.

In December of 2022 I decided to retire completely from my part-time consulting work. Even though I loved the ranch risk assessments, they dominated my schedule and were beginning to interfere with doctor appointments and other personal events. We wanted to do some traveling together to go some places Debbi had never been. I finished my last field work in mid-December. With Christmas coming up, I really didn't notice the change in time available. Debbi and I got involved in a Bible study group that met every other Wednesday night. Tom Cunningham and I started a Thursday morning men's Bible study group at our church. I began doing a lot more jigsaw puzzles and walking the dogs more. But I was still wondering what God wanted me to do.

On January 19, 2023, I had an appointment with my primary care physician to simply catch up on happenings since my last visit with her. She was in the background now that I was seeing the oncologist. I did ask her what she thought of me doing some exercises or going to a gym because I thought my muscles were reducing in size. She agreed it would be a good idea, and recommended I go to a physical therapist instead because they would know more about my condition. She added that stronger muscles would use blood oxygen more efficiently, which might help with my persistent fatigue.

DONOR SEARCH

On January 24, I drove the 150-mile round trip to Dallas so they could draw more blood to search for a bone marrow donor. We were not sure why they would begin the search now, when it could be several years before we would have to decide about a transplant, but we figured they knew the scheduling better than us.

I was starting to pay attention to my body more and we were making a list of questions to ask my oncologist the next time we met. For a while, I had pain in one of my ankles and pain in my hip/pelvic area every morning when I got out of bed. One of the symptoms of primary myelofibrosis is bone pain, so I kept notes when the pain would come and go. I was hoping it was simply being 69 years old.

On January 30, I went for my first physical therapy visit and initial evaluation. The therapist came up with an exercise routine for me to try at home. I would go back once a week to see how I was doing. I had to pay $25 copay for each session, so she thought we could start off with weekly visits while I do the daily exercises on my own. The next few days I did all the exercises at home and found it was tough for me to get down on the floor and back up for some of them, so I decided to go see if the YMCA or some other gym had an elevated platform from which I could do them.

This same day, Debbi just lost control of her emotions and confessed that she was mad and sad and scared about me dying from cancer. We hugged and talked a lot about how she was feeling, and we agreed that she should take advantage of some of the counseling resources we had at our church. I think it is important to note this because it was so easy to focus on myself and how I was dealing with this and not know how Debbi (my wife AND caregiver) was dealing with it. I needed to keep a better lookout for her emotions, and she needed to be honest about how she felt and not try to hide or bottle up or push down her feelings. So, my advice to others who must go through this would be honesty and transparency. Two over-used words maybe, but if you aren't both forthcoming with your feelings you are just going to put your relationship at a disadvantage (my $0.02 worth).

We were "iced in" January 31 and February 1 because of freezing weather and rain, so we had lots of time inside the house. I found a Facebook myelofibrosis private support group of people who have or had MF. It turned out to be a wealth of information, including people's stories about their experiences, treatments, struggles with doctors, and personal accounts of long-term treatments and successful and unsuccessful transplants. We spent a lot of time reading people's posts on the site, and it really shed some light on some of the topics we had been wondering about. One more example of how there are many resources available for self-education on this and other diseases.

We spent most of the month of February waiting. I continued going to a physical therapist and joined the YMCA so I could do some daily exercises to improve muscle tone, which I thought would improve the efficiency with which my muscles use the available oxygen in my blood.

On February 8, more blood work was done by my hematologist to monitor my basic blood components. On February 23 a CT scan was done to compare my spleen size to previous scans. In some cases, the spleen will try to produce red blood cells when the bone marrow no longer produces as many as needed. This causes the spleen to enlarge, and in some cases the spleen must be removed to prevent it from bursting. This didn't happen in my case.

March 1 was our second meeting with the transplant doctor in Dallas. I went to the lab first so blood could be taken for analysis and continued comparisons.

Waiting seems to be what we were doing the most of now. We waited nearly an hour past our appointment time, but the doctor immediately apologized, saying he had gotten tied up with the previous patient. After some preliminary "how are you feeling" questions, he got straight to the point. The very expensive and extensive lab analysis of my most recent blood samples revealed two additional mutations: ASXL1 and U2AF1. Both were "high risk" factors, and he explained that he now recommended a bone marrow transplant within the next six months to one year. This was quite a change in urgency compared to our visit 90 days ago. Additionally, he said the donor search had resulted in one match (noting that usually it was thousands). He printed out detailed information about the two additional mutations, said they would be verifying the match of the donor, and would see us again in 90 days.

It took a while for this new information to sink in while driving back home to Granbury. Our mindset was no longer "if we need a transplant someday." It was now "we need a transplant within the next 6-12 months." Life goes on . . . but now it included a higher level of anxiety, knowing a bone marrow transplant has evolved from "maybe" to "definitely".

I called and talked with the transplant coordinator with my health insurance company. I told her we were concerned that only one match had been found! She said there are always more than a single match, and the doctor probably meant "a" good match and not "one" good match. She assured me he would not even consider a questionable match. She also noted that related donors are not normally considered due to heredity. She shared details about the pre-transplant work-up that begins when he feels a transplant is imminent and said she would put a 3-ring binder in the mail with all the details regarding transplants. The binder arrived via FedEx the next day, and Debbi and I began reading sections of it every day.

Friends and relatives were naturally curious and continued to pray for me. They wanted to know more about the donor search, and all I could tell them was that we would meet with the transplant doctor again on June 1st – and until then, we waited.

I received a cheek swab kit in the mail, followed the directions, and sent it back the next day. More DNA marker testing, we were told, yet another means to find a donor. No stone unturned.

It was now April 2023, five months since I received the MF diagnosis, although we knew I'd had it longer because my previous blood work showed evidence of low red blood cell counts, or anemia. I still didn't have any serious symptoms. I was tired a lot more often and

I had aches and pains, but they came and went, so we weren't sure they were directly related to the MF.

I didn't dwell on the cancer every day. It didn't do any good to worry about it because there wasn't any part I could control. I was actively involved in church activities like Bible study groups and continued to do my exercises, walk the dogs, and ride my motorcycle more now that the weather was better. The week after my 70th birthday we went on a group motorcycle ride in the Texas Hill Country with some of my long-time motorcycling buddies. It was the best five days I'd had in a long time. I was able to fill the guys in on my cancer, but the best part of the week was just riding, traveling, and enjoying the wildflowers and friendships, especially with Debbi, who had not been on a group motorcycle ride before.

When we returned home, one of the riders let us know that she had tested positive for COVID. Her husband also tested positive a couple of days later. I immediately tested myself, and it was negative. Debbi and I both had runny noses from allergies during the trip and afterward, but never did run a fever or have any respiratory problems or other COVID-related symptoms. Glad we didn't get it!

Later in April, I participated in a pharmaceutical company advertising study. I initially did a short phone interview with the third-party recruiter, who verified I was in a high-risk category for MF. I filled out some questionnaires about my MF diagnosis, symptoms, and what stage of treatment I was in. The study was basically to determine my reaction to several advertising images and messages about a new drug the company had developed to "enhance" the effectiveness of another drug that had been on the market for several years. Since I wasn't taking any treatment drugs for my MF, a lot of the questions didn't apply to me directly, but they were happy with my participation and opinions . . . and I got paid to participate. It would be interesting if I saw advertisements I recognized in a magazine in the future.

When Debbi and I met, I had been traveling full-time for several years. I missed the travel a lot. I wanted to take Debbi places she'd never been and show her some of my favorites. Places where I've watched sunrises and sunsets in the mountains and along streams where had

I felt so close to God in the middle of His creation. Looming in the back of my mind were thoughts that we may run out of time to travel together. The last week of April, we went on another trip, this time to Colorado. We drove from Granbury to Amarillo and spent the first night there. The next day we traveled to Eagle Nest and Taos, NM where we did some sightseeing and spent the night. From there, we drove north to Alamosa alongside the Sangre De Cristo Mountains range to Poncha Springs, Salida, and Buena Vista, Colorado. A winter storm had come through ahead of us and had dumped a LOT of snow. Well, what was considered a lot to us Texans. The timing was just perfect, because we could see it snowing in the mountains around us and we drove through some flurries, but we had dry roads with beautiful snow-covered landscapes and mountain views. We continued to Leadville and Frisco, where we picked up I-70 East. We got off the interstate at Idaho Springs and took Highway 6 to Golden, where we spent the night. We had breakfast at an Italian bakery the next morning and met with the owner of the company I had worked for at a coffee shop near her home (the first time I had ever met her in person). We spent a couple of days visiting my son Adam and his friend Cordelia, stayed in Adam's downtown Denver loft home, and had a great time eating out at different restaurants, shopping at the local Orvis and flagship R.E.I. stores and just catching up. We returned to Granbury via a direct route along US 287 back through Amarillo. The trip was a great mini-vacation and a good distraction from medical issues.

In late April, I began having pains in my left hip and in my lower abdominal area. The hip pain would come and go, but the abdominal pain continued to increase and became constant, increasing when I bent over forward to tie my shoes or pick up after the dogs on our walks. On May 19 I had a CT scan ordered by my oncologist's office to try and pinpoint the source of my abdominal pain. The most likely source was from further enlargement of my spleen, but the pain was much lower than where the spleen is located. At the last minute, the tech told me the scan needed to be WITH contrast, so I drank the Barium solution. The scan went smoothly and quickly and as I was getting ready to leave the tech asked me why it had been ordered. I explained the pain I was having, and she was surprised and said the scan was ordered for my UPPER abdomen! She called the doctor's office to see if they wanted to order another scan since I was already there, and they said no.

Two days later, the results were posted onto my patient portal and the notes were made by an MD who interpreted the images. The findings as noted were very confusing because they said that no oral contrast was used and that wasn't true – I drank the Barium solution right before the scan. And the spleen measurement comparison was not correct!

I scheduled a doctor appointment with a P.A. at my primary care physician's office in Fort Worth. He poked on me and manipulated my left leg and ordered a urinalysis, blood lab work, X-Ray of my left hip, and CT scans with and without contrast of my pelvic and lower abdominal area. He was confident the hip pain was due to bursitis, so he prescribed prednisone and X-Rays to follow up. Not sure about the abdominal pain, he ordered CT scans, which were scheduled for May 31.

In two days, my hip pain was gone. I continued to take the prednisone as prescribed. The lab results came in, and my red blood cell count, white blood cell count, and platelets all remained lower than normal, but had not changed dramatically in the last few months. The urinalysis was normal. On May 31, I had X-Rays taken of my hip and CT scans with and without contrast. The kidney tests the tech did before the scans came back normal – no kidney issues – good news! The next day we were to go see the transplant doctor in Dallas.

I thanked God every day that I didn't have any debilitating or painful symptoms. Considering the seriousness of my prognosis, I continued to have good quality of life. All my life I have been an optimist, always thinking there is a silver lining on every cloud. I have always looked forward, not backward. I love the quote "There is a reason the rear-view mirror is so small, and the windshield is so large – where you are going is more important than where you have been."

I never dreamed I would have so much time to think about dying. And therein lies one of the biggest challenges of having a life-threatening disease or illness: time spent waiting, thinking and worrying. My thoughts and emotions kept bouncing all over the map. The doctor appointments and blood work kept reminding me that my days may be numbered. When I was confronted with the medical details, I began thinking about control – what was I going to do with my remaining days? How many more dreams can I try and accomplish? How can I prepare and try to make things as easy as possible for Debbi when I'm gone? How will I say goodbye to my wife and kids and friends? If you find yourself in this situation and asking these questions, I encourage you to remember the scripture

"Be anxious for nothing, but in everything by prayer and supplication, with thanksgiving, let your requests be made known to God; and the peace of God, which surpasses all understanding, will guard your hearts and minds through Christ Jesus." Philippians 4:6-7, NKJV

I believe this scripture reminds us that it does us no good to ponder our problems. We can choose what to focus on, and we should choose to be thankful for our blessings, not our problems. When Peter was walking on the water toward Jesus, while he focused on Jesus, he was OK. But when he took his eyes off Jesus and focused on the water, he began to sink. We need to remember God is the controller of all things. He doesn't need our help. Our anxiety doesn't fix anything, it just uses up our energy. We need to pray for God's help and give the problems to Him. I heard a sermon once where the preacher compared leaving worry with God to leaving your broken vacuum cleaner at the repair shop. We don't need to stay and help the repair person fix the problem. We need to leave it with him.

Our calendar was now filling up with doctor appointments and/or tests nearly every day. On June 1, we went to our appointment with the transplant doctor. I went to the lab first and they drew blood to get current readings. By the time we met with the doctor, he had the lab results. This answered two of our lingering questions – why did we always have to wait so long between the lab and seeing the doctor, and why did we have to wait for our next 90-day appointment to get lab results? Turns out he wasn't referring to 90-day old lab results at all each time we met with him, but current information obtained just a few minutes before.

My blood work was remaining stable, he said. He repeated that we need to go with a bone marrow transplant within six months to a year and seemed surprised that we had not been updated on the donor search. He said he would have the Transplant Coordinator contact me right away with the status of a donor, which he thought had been found and he commented that he had likely signed off with his approval. He felt around my abdomen, checked my heartbeat and breathing, and again said "see you in 90 days". We left with optimism that a donor had been found and we just hadn't been told yet.

The next Monday, I met with my local oncologist, who looked at the updates to my records on his computer and without much eye contact said he didn't think we needed two cooks in the kitchen, there wasn't anything he could contribute now that I was on the path to a transplant, and I didn't need to meet with him any longer. In a way, this was a relief because he hadn't been involved in my visits in the past several months. But in another way, it felt like a door had somehow been slammed shut.

Two days later, the Transplant Coordinator in Dallas called while Debbi and I were eating lunch at a cafe near Ranger, TX. I stepped outside to get out of the noisy dining room and talked with her. She said two good donor matches had appeared on the BeTheMatch database, but when they followed up, they discovered the donors were no longer available. UP went my hopes and emotions, and then DOWN they immediately went again. I cried right there on the sidewalk. She then said they had located a "9 of 10" match and were checking on that donor. UP go my hopes again. She also asked about my siblings, and I told her Phyllis and Patrick were the youngest, but they were both over 50 years old. She said if they were very good matches, they might be used for backups in the event the match they found didn't work out. I told her I would contact Phyllis and Patrick and send here their contact information as soon as we got home.

When I went back in the café to tell Debbi about the phone call, she began asking me questions about the two donors, why they were no longer available, what happened to them and could the coordinator find out? It was like throwing gasoline on a fire. She was upset because I couldn't answer all her questions and I was upset because I didn't have the answers, and we were soon nearly at each other's throats. All because of miscommunication, misunderstanding, and just plain stress. The meal was miserable, the trip back home was miserable. I texted Phyllis and Patrick, who were both happy about being tested and possibly being the donor. Later that afternoon, my emotions just boiled over. I began crying uncontrollably and couldn't stop. I don't remember a time when I was more frustrated or exhausted. We are in control of so few things when it comes to the entire process. We are at the mercy of the doctors and how much they do or don't communicate with us. The doctors are at the mercy of how the cancer progresses and who is in the donor database. Waiting results in anxiety, and anxiety leads to frustration, and frustration can lead to anger. All over things we cannot control.

I believe it is times like these when Satan will send demons to try and convince you that things are hopeless. In this case, Debbi and I began to take out our frustrations on each other. That's what the devil does; steal, kill, and destroy. He saw our anxiety and frustration as temporary weakness, tried to turn us against each other, attacked our marriage, and tried to get a foothold, hoping to push us away from God. But as we are told in the Bible, Christ gave Christians the authority to resist demons:

"Resist the devil, and he will flee from you." James 4:7, NKJV

Debbi and I snapped out of it. We agreed the only way we were going to get through this was to keep reminding ourselves that God is in control – not us. We decided we were going to get to thinking positive, that we were not going to obsess with the cancer all day every day and we were going to get back to enjoying life between doctor appointments. We prayed together and asked God to take over.

On June 8, I went to my primary care physician to check out a spot near my right ear that appeared to be like one I had on my chest several years ago that turned out to be basil cell carcinoma. The P.A. looked at it and referred me to a skin cancer center in Fort Worth. The soonest I could get an appointment was July 11ᵗʰ.

On June 13 the Transplant Coordinator called and said she would send a calendar of appointments for pre-transplant workup testing to be done on June 30.

On June 26 the Donor Coordinator called and said Phyllis and Patrick were both 7 of 10 matches at best. She said she had two donor matches she was following up on and should have some results early the next week.

On June 30 we were back in Dallas. We went to the lab in building D, and they took several tubes of blood for analysis. We then met with the financial counselor, signed forms agreeing to share my medical information because my case was now technically a "clinical trial" so Medicare would pay for my bone marrow transplant and related costs, which they originally denied. Then we went to building A for my pulmonary function test and echocardiogram, and back to building D to meet with the Transplant Coordinator. We still didn't have any details on the donor matches.

On July 5 the Transplant Coordinator called and said they needed me to come back to the hospital and give more blood samples for additional testing. I was out riding my motorcycle and was in Weatherford, TX when she called, and just headed straight for Dallas. They took 14 vials of blood this time. So glad it was with only one needle. I continued to thank God for every new day without any painful symptoms. Adam got his replacement swab kit from BeTheMatch and returned it the same day. I sent the Transplant Coordinator a text letting her know and that we had done the pre-transplant workup tests on the 30ᵗʰ. She texted me back right away and said she was aware of the completed tests and the additional blood work and would be following up with the results and keep me posted.

On July 10 I sent the Transplant Coordinator an email asking for any information she could provide about when/if a transplant would occur. She said she would contact the Donor Coordinator and let me know ASAP. I also had an appointment with my dermatologist that same day to do the surgery to remove the carcinoma near my right ear. What looked like a small area of cancer cells on the surface turned out to need surgery, which took 14 stitches to close.

On July 13 the Transplant Coordinator emailed and said they were meeting with the transplant doctor in five days. She hoped to have an update that afternoon. We traveled to South Carolina on a vacation trip July 13-23 and didn't hear anything from her. On July 24 I sent an email to the Transplant Coordinator asking for an update. She replied immediately and said she would confirm which chemotherapy regimen the transplant doctor planned to use. Different combinations of chemotherapy and/or radiation are used depending on the type of match between the donor and recipient. After that, she would request transplant approval, which takes 7-10 days. She said she would pencil in dates for my transplant while we waited for approval. My transplant doctor was continuing to watch my blood test results, but our waiting was nearly over.

By this time, I was in full speed "prepare in case" mode, thinking about things that would have to be done and things that would change immediately in Debbi's life if I were to die. We reviewed our Wills and Medical Directives and got them updated, something everyone should do even if they are perfectly healthy, because life on this earth can end in the blink of an eye, any day. One of the things I wanted to do was take Debbi somewhere she always wanted to go. Top of her list was the Biltmore Estate, in North Carolina. I planned a road trip that would take us from Granbury, TX to Ashville, NC to see the Biltmore, then to Charleston, SC for a couple of days, then a return route that would take us along the Gulf Coast. Debbi got to wade in the Atlantic Ocean and the Gulf of Mexico. We had a wonderful time, visiting places that almost completely took our minds off the cancer.

I began feeling a tug to attend seminary training. I remember tossing the idea around in my head for a while, and talking to some fellow Stonewater members who had attended seminary classes taught by Dr. Joey White, one of our senior pastors. One night, while walking the dogs around our neighborhood, I remember doubting I was young enough to attend seminary, wondering what benefit would it be for a 69-year-old to commit to two years of training, and would the money be better spent by just donating it to the church? I did a lot of praying while walking our dogs, and as I often do in my prayers, I repeated what pastor Jeremy White told me soon after I first met him: "Ask God to tell you what you need to know and tell you what you need to do." That night, I had a dream that I was sitting at my desk writing a check for the first seminary class. In September of 2023, I attended my first seminary class. This was another step in the strengthening of my faith. That dream was vivid. It was an answer to my prayers. I believe the Holy Spirit was speaking to me directly, telling me exactly what to do.

Now Or Never

My blood analysis results continued to reveal lower levels of critical components that indicated the myelofibrosis was continuing at a rate that prompted my transplant doctor to use the phrase "now or never". If we continued to wait, the fibrosis (scar tissue) would continue to a point where even a bone marrow transplant would not save my life. We assured the doctor we were "all in".

On November 26, at the Stonewater Church IMPACT group meeting, Pastor James Marcum's message was about the power of prayer. After his message, members of the group stood together as a body of powerful prayer warriors, gathered around and laid hands on me, anointed me with oil, and prayed for healing. This was a very emotional experience for me.

> "Is anyone among you sick? Let him call for the elders
> of the church, and let them pray over him, anointing
> him with oil in the name of the Lord. And the prayer
> of faith will save the sick, and the Lord will raise him
> up. And if he has committed sins, he will be forgiven."
> James 5:14-15, NKJV

During the month of November, the transplant coordinator developed a "transplant calendar" that included the dates of each critical step in the transplant process. On November 29, we had an appointment with my transplant doctor to review the latest blood work and to sign several consent forms related to the transplant. During this meeting, the doctor reviewed the risks involved, reiterated that my chance of survival through the initial chemotherapy was about 60%, and then looked at Debbi, pointed his finger, and said "If your husband is salvageable, I need your commitment that you will let me salvage him". The word "salvage" shocked both of us. The doctor explained that the reason he brought this up was because sometimes there were complications during the initial chemotherapy and transplant. In the past, a few wives had stopped treatments in the middle of the process because they did not want to see their husbands suffer any longer. Debbi confidently confirmed that she was "all in" and we were not about to give up in the middle of the treatments. We drove back home that afternoon knowing that we had now transitioned from watch and wait mode to life-saving mode. On December 16, I discontinued taking the blood thinner to reduce the risk of blood clots. I would not be taking a blood thinner during the transplant process.

Bill proposing to Debbi

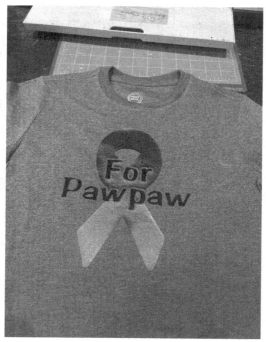

Beau and Luke's T-shirts for Cancer Awareness Day at school

ALLOGENEIC PERIPHERAL BLOOD STEM CELL TRANSPLANT CALENDAR FOR Billy Greenwade (Myelofibrosis)

December 2023

Sunday	Monday	Tuesday	Wednesday	Thursday	Friday	Saturday
3	4 Donor Collects Stem Cells!	5	6	7	8	9
10	11	12	13	14	15	16 No ASPIRIN products starting today for Broviac placement on Dec 21
17	18	19	20 Check In at 1 PM, Building A 1st Floor Admissions Chest Scan — Check In at 1:45 PM Building D, 4th Floor Labs — Check in at 2 PM Building D, 270 Admit Appt with Kala Rutledge PA	21 D-7 Nothing to eat or drink after 6 AM for line placement — Check In at 12 PM Bldg A, 1st Floor Admissions Central Line Placement — **Admit To Hospital Today**	22 D-6 Fludarabine (Chemo)	23 D-5 Fludarabine (Chemo)
24 D-4 Fludarabine (Chemo)	25 D-3 Fludarabine Melphalan (Chemo)	26 D-2 Fludarabine Melphalan (Chemo)	27 D-1 Rest Day	28 D0 Transplant Day!	29	30

Monday, December 04, 2023; SR

Transplant Calendar

Stonewater IMPACT group praying for Bill and Debbi

Bill and Debbi on hospital check-in day

Adam in from Denver for son-to-father support

Christmas Day 2023

One million donor stem cells ready for transplant

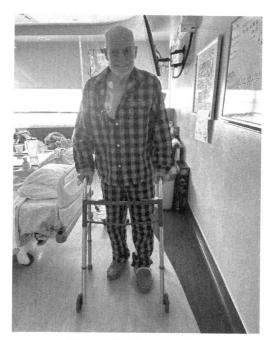

First walk after transplant

Hospital discharge day

Our hotel home away from home

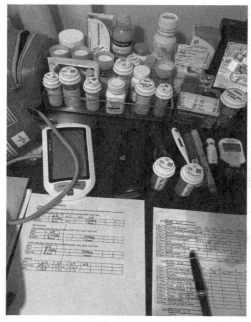

Keeping track of daily medications

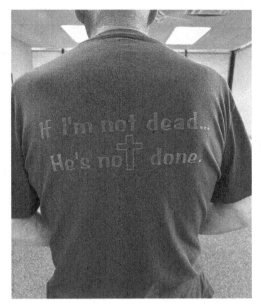

A favorite T-shirt

Bill's 71st birthday and his 1st after his transplant

Kneeling in prayer added to Bill's PT schedule

Back in Church

Celebrating our 4th wedding anniversary 2024

Transplant

December 20, 2023, we spent the day at the hospital in Dallas. I had a COVID test, completed admissions paperwork and more lab work was done. We had another meeting with the doctor who would be overseeing my chemotherapy and transplant. It was a long day! We walked over 2 miles inside the hospital complex. The tests went well. We stayed in a nearby hotel to avoid driving over 120 miles round trip home and back.

The next day we were told that during my hospitalization, visitors would be very limited – to one per day, plus Debbi. No visitors were allowed to "come and go" and would not be able to schedule ahead of time but would have to check with the nurses daily. The reason for these restrictions was because visitors are not allowed at all if I was having a severe reaction to the chemotherapy or was fighting life-threatening rejection after the transplant. There was no way to predict if that might happen. This was disappointing for our friends and family, but we had to respect the hospital's concern for safety. We were so grateful for all the prayers and support, and we promised to post updates on Facebook every day and send texts to those who were not Facebook users.

There was lots of paperwork and waiting Thursday. The surgery for placement of my central line catheter went well. My son Adam had traveled from Colorado, was good son-father support for me, and good company for Debbi in the waiting rooms. About 6pm, I was moved to my room in the transplant Intensive Care Unit. I felt things were now "real". My room had a large window, allowing me to see the outside world. Everything in the room was so clean and organized. In addition to my hospital bed, there was a recliner, a large TV, and a couch that folded out to a bed where Debbi could spend the night when she wanted.

Friday I was introduced to my "patient pal" for the next few weeks, an IV pole with wheels on the base. IV bags were hung from the pole and tubing connected from the IV bags to the ports in my chest. I learned very quickly to be careful getting in and out of bed without tangling or tugging on the IV lines from the pole to the ports. One of my friends said he named his IV pole "Wally." My "Wally" accompanied me everywhere. He went into the bathroom, waited on the other side of the shower curtain, and went on walks up and down the hall with me. There were always lengths of clear tubing connecting me and Wally.

My first chemotherapy infusion went well with no noticeable side effects. I couldn't believe it. I had heard so much about chemotherapy making people very sick. When the nurse inspected the incisions where my port was put in, he said "Wow, you don't have any bleeding at all! Impressive." I replied, "God is impressive, that's why."

The hallways on the transplant ICU floors formed a big square, with rooms around the perimeter and nurses' stations and supply rooms in the middle. Patients were encouraged to walk (with their IV pole in tow). 26 laps around the floor equaled 1 mile. I figured out it was hard to walk when the doctors were making their daily rounds (they always had several interns with them) or when housekeeping people were cleaning rooms, changing sheets, etcetera. 3:00pm was a good time to walk. I walked 3/4 mile in one session, for a total of 1.5 miles for the day.

Adam flew back home to Denver that Saturday. Before he left, he showed us how to watch football games on my iPad because the TV in my room was on the blink. Thank you, Adam. It seemed to always be cold in my room, but we had lots of blankets. And the food was better than any hospital food I'd ever eaten. My second chemotherapy session complete, I only had a touch of nausea. Thank you, Lord.

Christmas Eve was another successful day of chemotherapy, again with no side effects. When the doctor made his rounds, he checked my vitals and records and said, "very boring - that's good." I was already getting tired of the hospital bed, so I sat in the recliner while Debbi and

I watched the Dallas Cowboys game. I posted an update on Facebook and thanked everyone again for their prayers.

On Christmas Day, I woke up and thanked God for the day we celebrate the birth of Jesus. When my friend Jim Flaming called, he said "this will be a Christmas you'll remember." He was so right. I told him I had already opened my gift of another new day. I was done with chemotherapy infusion 5 of 7, the drug being notorious for causing mouth sores, so the nurses insisted patients chew ice before, during, and after the infusions. My mouth was so cold I could hardly talk - but I still chewed ice. And so far, I had no sores. We were so thankful for the constant flow of prayers from everyone. Merry Christmas!

December 26 was Day -2 (minus 2). By 2:30pm, both of my chemotherapy infusions were done! I had been chewing ice (and sugar-free popsicles) for hours...and so far, no mouth sores or nausea or any other side effects. Thank you, Lord. Next, I got an infusion of a chemical to prevent Graft Vs Host Disease, or GVHD (see page 31 for more details). The nurses then said I could take the rest of the day off, LOL.

Wednesday, December 27 was Day -1, the day before my transplant day, a rest day with no chemotherapy. I received several infusions and pills of anti-rejection drugs to begin preparing my body for the transplant cells from my donor. Still no side effects. Praise God! I even walked 1/2 a mile. It had been a good day. Debbi was back from her trip home for a couple of days. We were excited about tomorrow. It turned out to be a busy night, however. I developed a large blood clot in my left leg, had a CT scan, and a vascular surgeon was contacted to do surgery as soon as possible. This was not good. I now had no immune system. If I contacted the slightest infection during or after my leg surgery, it could mean the difference in life and death. For the first time, I was scared. Lying in that dark room, with only the sound of machines beeping occasionally, I started asking a lot of "what if?" questions in my mind. What if I get an infection in my leg while I have no immune system to fight it? What if they must do more surgery on my leg? What if the donor cells aren't a good enough match? What if, what if, what if? I had to remind myself that there was nothing I could do. I prayed and asked

God to calm my nerves, I asked Him to double-check everything the doctors and nurses were doing, and I asked Him to keep His promise that He would never leave me.

Day 0. My transplant was scheduled for 10:30am. One million stem cells were transplanted by IV, which took 4 hours, with an attending nurse in the room the entire time. Several nurses came into my room to wish me luck. The atmosphere was electric. December 29 was Day +1 in transplant terms. I thanked God every day for the Transplant Team. They were professional and very caring. Most were Believers, and I was working on the rest. Debbi had been by my side every step. I don't know what I would have done without her. I kept posting daily updates on Facebook and thanked everyone for their continuous prayers.

New Year's Eve - Day +3. The surgery to remove the blood clot in my left leg was performed right before midnight, was successful, and I was soon back in my room. I was given a unit of blood that morning, and I was being very closely monitored. Blood was taken for lab analysis every 4 hours to be sure I didn't have any type of infection. We continued to pray my new stem cells liked their new home. Happy New Year's Eve!

New Year's Day - Day +4. I don't remember a lot of the details of this day. Debbi posted this Facebook update: "For those who may not know yet, Bill has had a little setback from his blood clot surgery, but the surgeon thinks he's got it under control; there seems to be some internal bleeding at the surgery site. He has ordered more platelets to help with clotting and Bill is on oxygen as well. Bill is having pain with all of this, but they are giving him pain meds to deal with that as well. He's a trooper and says this is just a bump in the road. I want to thank each and every one of you who are continuing to pray for us through this entire process. We feel them. This part is totally unrelated to his cancer treatment. The transplanted stem cells will take 2-3 weeks to attach and start working. I'll send updates on any new changes."

January 2, Day +5...the sunrise was beautiful from my hospital room. Post-transplant signs were still trending positive. I received several anti-rejection drugs, and my vital signs were monitored every hour. My transplant doctor made his morning rounds and was pleased with the progress so far. My leg remained the focus of concern. It was still very swollen and painful, so we were keeping it elevated. I was getting blood and platelets infusions to address the internal bleeding. The vascular surgeon was cautiously optimistic that he would not have to do corrective surgery. I was learning to sleep in 1-hr segments between tests and infusions. I even slept through one of my blood draws. The nurses and doctors were top notch. I was determined to keep counting my blessings and not my complaints. At this point, I hadn't lost any of my hair. In fact, I was growing a transplant beard.

January 3, Day +6. Breakfast was a buffet of my normal medications, plus anti-viral, anti-rejection, and pain medications. The magic of chemistry. My white blood cell count had been 0.0 for 3 days now. At noon, I got my first injection of a protein that stimulates bone marrow to produce white blood cells from the new stem cells and release them into the bloodstream. I would get these shots daily. I was able to move my leg and tried to increase the range of motion, hoping the swelling would go down soon.

Just a few days after my transplant, our dear friends Roy and Tricia Bullard walked into my room. I was so surprised and filled with emotion when I saw them. We had a very nice visit, and they prayed over me while there. It was very special to see them.

On one of my walks, one of the other patients in the ICU and I were talking and sharing why we were there, what kind of cancer we had, when we had our transplants, and what our status was. Into the conversation, he asked, "How can you be so calm?" and started to break down. This was one of my earliest opportunities to share my faith while in the hospital. I told him how I had given my challenge to God, and about the peace I had experienced ever since. I listened, and he shared doubts about his future. He asked me more questions, and I shared scripture with him I thought pertained to his fears. I never got another chance to talk to him because our paths didn't cross again, but prayed for him and hoped he would find some peace and would lean on his faith as I had.

January 4 - Day +7. I had heard many stories about physical therapy people whose job it seems is to hurt you. Now I could relate. I was able to take some steps using a walker, and my physical therapist was going to make sure I walked more steps every day. Making his rounds, my doctor said, "everything is as expected, except for your leg." But it was getting better, with the swelling going down slowly.

By mid-afternoon, I could walk WITHOUT the walker, albeit at a snail's pace. My vitals remained stable, and I had no signs of infection or rejection so far.

> "Is anyone among you suffering? Let him pray. Is anyone cheerful? Let him sing psalms." James 5:13, NKJV

Debbi and I were praying and signing. January 5 - Day +8 was uneventful, which is how my doctors and nurses liked things. Debbi and I remained grateful that I still had no complications related to my transplant. This was the first day I could walk more than a few steps since I had the surgery on my leg. I walked (with a walker) a full lap around the floor. We were so blessed to have so many friends and family praying for us!

January 6 - Day +9. I didn't have much to report that day. No surprises, no drama, slow and steady. My vitals remained constant. I was still getting blood infusions and medications and trying to increase exercise. I walked nearly a mile, some of it without my walker! The nurses on my floor worked twelve-hour shifts and they rotated weekends off, so I met a lot of different nurses. One day my nurse introduced herself as Faith. I told her what a beautiful name I thought it was. I asked her "How is your faith, Faith?" She said she was a believer who was raised in a Christian home, but she had questions. I just knew God wasn't waiting for my transplant to be over to put me to work. Faith and I were able to have several opportunities for me to listen and discuss her questions and share my faith. God at work through me.

January 7 – Day +10. We were in double digits on days now! The only known side effects I had were the persistent GI tract problem and now sores in my mouth. They were giving me Imodium to address the Gastrointestinal tract problem. The only way to drink or eat anything without pain (imagine salt in a sore) was to get it past my lips first.

I'll never make fun of a sippy cup again. Early that morning, I went out to the little kitchen area and made a fresh pot of coffee. While it was brewing, I walked by the nurses' stations and said good morning. One of the nurses said, "Here's the man with the Spirit." I asked, "The Holy Spirit, right?" and they smiled. I share this because the past month among so many new strangers had made me realize how many opportunities we are given to share our faith. We can choose to sit and be quiet or get up and be active. I know everyone isn't an extrovert, but if you'll just muster a little courage to talk to others, God will help you with what to say. Or you can just listen! I thanked God every day for saving my life through the generosity of the bone marrow donor and the prayers of so many. I was happy to share how good He is.

The blood draw taken at midnight that night showed that my white blood cell count had changed from 0.0 to 0.1! That meant my new stem cells had started making white blood cells. We had beaten the odds. My nurse, cautioning that everybody is different, said this normally happens around day 12. So, I was two days ahead of average. Hallelujah! She said, "this is impressive" and my reaction was again "Our God is impressive!"

January 8 – Day +11. One of the nurses asked me "now that you've been in the hospital for over two weeks, what do you miss the most?" My answer was "my people". I missed my church family. The day had been a good one. PT had gone well with their exercise suggestions, and I was gaining mobility in my leg. I walked 1.1 miles the day before and my new goal was 2.2 miles. The sores in my mouth were less, not more. My WBC had gone from 0.0 to 0.1 to 0.2 in three days. My ANC had gone from 0.0 to 0.09 (this was a big deal). The head nurse said he rarely saw this, and if it continued, I would leave the hospital in two weeks! I got infusions of platelets, magnesium, and more anti-rejection drugs. We weren't out of the woods yet. I was so thankful for everyone's prayers! We were so fortunate to have so many people supporting us.

January 9 – Day + 12. Every time I experienced a new symptom that I thought was out of the ordinary (nosebleed, difficulty swallowing) I let my nurse in charge know. They either had an immediate solution or said, "no big deal – try to go back to sleep". A clump of my hair that had fallen out from the chemotherapy was one of those situations, LOL. We felt like this day was one of the best days yet. Blood was drawn at midnight and lab results were posted on the whiteboard in my room. My white blood cell count increased from 0.2 to 0.4, and my ANC went from 0.09 to 0.29. My pain medications had been reduced to half what I was previously taking, and my leg continued to get better – I was walking more steps every day.

My sister Phyllis called to let me know our mother had died. She had fallen at home and had been in the hospital in Arlington for surgeries related to injuries from the fall. We had both undergone surgeries, and she was in and out of consciousness for several days. Phyllis would relay messages between us, but we didn't get to speak to each other during her last days. I felt helpless, but I also knew God was watching over both of us. He knew what He was doing.

I had two nurses ask me if I was a preacher, and I told them no, but I was working on it. I was so grateful that even on the hospital transplant floor, I had opportunities to share my faith. Some of my friends said I was amazing...I wasn't, I just stepped aside and let God reveal His plan, trusted and obeyed. I didn't know how anyone could go through this without faith, a supportive family, church family and friends who call, write, text, and pray without ceasing. If you are suffering, do your best to stay in touch with friends and family. Make new friends when you have opportunities. Isolation will only give you more time to worry about your condition.

January 10, Day +13. Debbi bought a "snow angel" before Christmas and she kept us company in the hospital room. She was a sweet reminder to be grateful, read my Bible and pray. Every time we changed the number of "+" days, I was amazed at the bone marrow transplant process. There are SO many factors involved, and the hospital staff had implemented God's plan beautifully. The lab results from the blood draw at midnight showed that my WBC increased again, from 0.4 to 0.6 and my ANC rose from 0.29 to 0.48, both signs the new stem cells were at work.

The vascular team was happy with the progress on my leg (had to keep up the PT). That morning my transplant doctor said if it weren't for the slow healing of my leg, he would release me to go home. Since we would have to come to the doctor's office two or three times a week for a while, "home" would be a nearby hotel to keep us from driving so far. And if there were complications, we needed to be minutes from the hospital, not hours. So, the transplant had been a success! In my daily updates, I thanked every one of my family and friends who had been by our sides.

January 11 – Day +14. At 8:00am, my vascular surgeon came by, looked at my leg, and said to unwrap it and begin using a Ted hose, which applies more even pressure over the entire length of my leg. I had vegetable soup for supper the night before, scrambled eggs and bacon for breakfast that morning, and both promptly ended up in the trash can (better than all over me!) I had stomach cramps and nausea all day, and finally got steroids to help. I was certainly not complaining...God had been so good to me. These were just some of the bumps in the road we had to get over. On one of my walks, I heard a nurse say, "she has only been awake once and said one word", referring to another patient. Debbi met a man in the hall whose father had been in the ICU over 40 days with leukemia. I hoped I would have a chance to discuss faith with these patients. I kept walking and trying to exercise my leg, mentally thanking everyone for their prayers.

January 12 – Day +15. My white blood cell count was up to 1.0, and my ANC was up to 0.89. These numbers were so good. The vascular surgeon's PA came at 8:00am, removed the Ted hose and re-wrapped my leg, saying she was happy with the progress and to stay on it as much as I could tolerate. It seemed my newest challenge was now nutrition. I couldn't keep food down. The nurses were giving me anti-nausea medication, which wasn't working. Most of my "walking" was now bed to bathroom, but I was determined to get out in the hallway. A case manager interviewed me for beginning discharge steps and went over the list of medications I'd be taking when I went home. A nurse checked my blood glucose. It was over 200, so she gave me an insulin shot right before supper. We hoped the high glucose level was due to the steroids I was taking for various things and was not a permanent situation.

January 13 – Day +16. My transplant doctor met with us the night before, still making his rounds at 10:30pm. He said he planned to discharge me on Monday or Tuesday. My new medications I would be taking had been ordered for pickup at Walgreens downstairs on Monday. During 6:00am rounds, my head nurse updated my lab results: WBC was up to 1.7, HGB was up to 8.0, platelets were up to 16,000, and ANC was up 66% to 1.48. I tried to get out of my hospital bed and room as often as possible, to combat cabin fever and get some walking exercise. I had to take my IV pole along with me, so I wasn't a speedster. On one occasion, a graduate student of one of the seminary schools came by and asked if he could visit and pray for me. He was a volunteer at the hospital, and I got to ask him about his experiences. I had been feeling a tug to maybe volunteer in hospitals, nursing homes, or other health facilities. Maybe I would pursue that tug when I got well enough. We praised our God in Heaven.

January 15 – Day +18. A new day, another gift. I slept well. I was up and down a few times, but not with my usual problem, so that was an improvement. I got up at 6:30am and walked to get a cup of coffee, which I hadn't had in four days. One of the choices was Southern Pecan – BINGO! My first cup was lukewarm. I thought about telling a nurse somebody ought to make a fresh pot. Remembering pastor Joey's advice about changing "somebody oughta" to "I oughta", I made a fresh pot myself. I had three main goals for the day: walk, walk, and walk. Walking would help my leg get better faster and would also help with my blood glucose. It was still high, so I was getting a needle stick in a finger (ouch) and an insulin shot before every meal. It was funny how the finger sticks hurt more than the shots. That morning my insulin dose was down from four units to three, so that was good. My transplant doctor said he suspected my GI tract problems were GVHD related, so they planned to huddle with specialists on Monday, and I would probably have a colonoscopy Tuesday. My weight was now down to 191 from 206. I was determined this was going to be a good day. Debbi and I thanked God for all our blessings.

In the hallway that morning, I met another patient, and we walked together for a while. There were scales in the hallway, and we were encouraged to weigh ourselves regularly. I had lost 15 pounds...my new friend Tom had lost over 45 pounds. He had received a bone marrow transplant about two months prior for leukemia and was back for treatment of GVHD in his gut. We talked about how our cancers were found, how we had been so well cared for by the hospital staff, and we talked the longest about our faith.

My doctors had decided to do a "mini colonoscopy" the next day, which meant I didn't have to drink the yucky stuff. Nothing to eat or drink after midnight, and I got three infusions of platelets that night. It was a good day. I finished my Lego project, completed two sessions of my seminary class on "Hearing God", and walked nearly a mile in the hallway.

January 16 – Day +19. It was hard to believe I had been in the hospital for 27 days, and today was 19 days since my transplant. Despite a few bumps in the road, my doctors were very pleased with my progress. The colonoscopy went well that morning. The doctor said things looked normal, and we would get lab results the next day. I seemed to finally have my appetite back and ate a big lunch. I was getting more calls and having more meetings with hospital staff about preparations for going home. A pharmacy representative reviewed the list of medications I would be taking for GVHD prevention, infection prevention, blood clot prevention, and other controls. I was told my "co-pay" for these would be about $500 per month…so glad we had the means to afford it…and thank God for Medicare. Another rep said she was ordering a diabetes meter and would be training me how to use it and give myself insulin injections. I was hoping this would be temporary. The steroids I was taking to help prevent GVHD also raised my blood glucose level, which required insulin, like a domino effect. The more my new stem cells accepted my body, the fewer steroids I would need; therefore the less insulin I would need. I needed to concentrate on not getting even the slightest cold or infection and things would be good. The plan for the day was to walk, read my Bible, walk some more, get some rest, and walk some more. My doctor was making his rounds later. I would have some more accurate information about when I could go home. I got on Facebook and again thanked everyone for their prayers, friendships, and fellowship.

January 17 – Day +20. My daughter Karen sent me photos of T-shirts she made for my grandsons Beau and Luke to wear to school on cancer awareness day. It had the cancer ribbon and said, "For PawPaw". At 5:30am I woke up dreaming about scripture and was wide awake. I got my Bible out and found myself in the book of Matthew. At 6:00am my nurse came in to start an IV for medications and a unit of blood. When she saw my Bible open, she began asking questions. We got into such a deep conversation that her supervisor called and reminded her that she had other patients to care for.

My transplant doctor was still making his rounds at 11:00pm. I don't know how they work so many hours. He liked my numbers (WBC up to 3.3 and ANC up to 2.84). We would get the biopsy report that day which would determine if I could go onto pill form steroids instead of IV. That would be a big step towards going home. Debbi was coming back today with empty suitcases. I was so glad she was home in Granbury during the cold weather, but I missed her! I was sure she missed sleeping on the couch in my room and the nurses coming in and out all night.

January 18 – Day +21. I got a new blue cloth bag filled with medical supplies and prescriptions. The diabetes trainer came by my room and showed me how to monitor my blood glucose (finger stick four times each day) and how to figure out how many units of insulin I would need depending on the glucose level. She trained me how to give myself insulin injections before each meal. The steroids I was taking to fight the GVHD would cause an increase in my blood glucose as long as I was taking them, like Type 2 diabetes. Hopefully, this would reverse when I was able to stop taking the steroids. Debbi got back, and I was sure happy to see her. In my current condition, we were not even able to kiss each other because of the possibility of sharing germs and me getting an infection. We were looking forward to when that stage would be over!

At 8:00pm, the vascular surgeon examined my leg and approved my discharge. There was still a lot of healing needed, but I was able to take full strides and no longer needed pain medication. The hospital transplant PA visited and reviewed procedures for follow up visits to the hospital. At first, we would be going to the clinic three times a week for blood work to monitor the GVHD and adjust medications. We had to go often because things could change so rapidly. My transplant doctor made his rounds early, changed some of my medications, and approved my discharge the next day. I was on the verge of tears saying goodbye to some of the nurses who had cared for me and had been so kind to me and Debbi.

January 19 – Day +22. The day started early, with platelet and blood transfusions at 5:00am. My hemoglobin and platelet levels needed to be good before I could be discharged, and both were now in range. Breakfast came at 7:30am. My blood glucose was 154, lower than the day before and I didn't require as much insulin before my meal. At 8:00am, my vitals were good. So far, "all systems go" as NASA used to say before a launch. At 8:30am, another blood draw was done for lab analysis. Man, I was loving my tri-fusion port system that eliminated the need for IV needles! The nurses changed the dressing on it so I would have a new one when I was discharged. The clinic and lab would continue to use the port system for months to come. There had been a constant flow of nurses, case managers, medication trainers, and doctors in my room throughout the day, training me and Debbi on next steps and responsibilities. Later that afternoon, a nurse brought a large cart up to my room, we loaded it full of our belongings and Debbi towed suitcases on wheels down to the lobby. Debbi retrieved our car from the parking garage. The nurse helped get me and all our stuff into the car, hugged us both, and wished us well.

We were out of the hospital, but we were not going home yet. The hospital and my insurance company had negotiated reduced rates with several hotels near the hospital for transplant patients who lived long distances away and would need a temporary "home away from home". We knew this ahead of time from the excellent training and materials provided months before my transplant. Debbi and I had visited some of the hotels on the list and decided on the Residence Inn because it had a kitchen, full-size refrigerator and a door separating the kitchen/living room area from the bedroom/bathroom area. It was surreal being out in the world again after a month in ICU, even if we were very limited how far we could go. It was just going to be a long road back to normal. In my daily Facebook updates, I continued to thank everyone again for their friendship, fellowship, and prayers.

Debbi and I both slept SO well that first night. I got up at 6:30am, checked my vitals (temperature, heart rate, blood pressure and blood glucose), gave myself an insulin shot, and made some coffee. I made breakfast and took my morning medications. Debbi got up early, washed clothes, unpacked hospital stuff and started a crockpot of vegetable soup. Then, when I was putting a sock on my left foot, blood spurted from my leg incision! It was like something you might see in a movie. It spurted more than three feet from where I was sitting. I immediately put pressure on it, Debbi got me some gauze, and I wrapped it tightly. We called the vascular surgeon, and he said get to the emergency room as soon as possible and have them call him as soon as they could assess it. We quickly got dressed, drove to the ER, and a CT scan was done. Then we waited and waited and waited. It turned out the bleeding was from a hematoma under the skin around the surgery site, and the pressure found a spot to release. It was determined I had good blood flow in my leg vessels and there was no need for more surgery. THANK YOU, LORD. We were soon back in our hotel room in Dallas near the hospital. Blood work was scheduled for the next day. That was quite a scare!

I reported to the lab at 8:30am Sunday. Debbi dropped me off at the hospital, blood was taken, sent to the lab, and I waited until they determined if I needed a transfusion. That morning, I got a good lab report. No need for a transfusion. Debbi picked me up. We planned to take it easy the rest of the day and maybe watch a football game on TV.

After a month of nurses waking me up at 4:00am, I think my body got used to it. I was up and wide awake at 4:00am Monday morning. We had a day off, with no doctor or hospital appointments. We were settling into our hotel suite and decided to try pre-ordering groceries online and picking them up outside the store to avoid the exposure of going inside.

After checking my vitals and blood glucose, I gave myself insulin shots and tried breakfast at the hotel continental breakfast area. I got there at 6:00am and discovered they didn't start serving until 6:30. Instead of walking back to our room, I got a cup of coffee and for 30 minutes the front desk manager and I talked about Jesus and how good our God is. It was a good time to share our faith at the beginning of the day. At 6:30, the cooks and I were the only ones there, so no worries about exposure to others. The food was delicious. I wore my mask to walk in the hallways to and from the breakfast area and took it off only while eating. I finished my seminary class online that day, so now I could write and submit my paper. I walked over two miles back and forth in the hotel hallways that day.

On January 23 Debbi and I went to the hotel breakfast area together, and she dropped me off at Medical City for lab work at 9:00. I walked to building D, where they drew blood, sent it to the lab, and I waited for the doctor to get the results. All my lab results were good, except for magnesium. The doctor discussed some adjustments to my oral medications, and that I would be getting an infusion of only magnesium. By this time, it was 11:00am. I walked from the office area back to the infusion area and was told because there were so many patients waiting, I would be going to building C for my infusion. I walked to building D pharmacy to pick up a new prescription, and then to building C, which is 0.65 miles via the maze of hallways. My magnesium infusion took 1-1/2 hours. From there, I walked to the main building A exit and called Debbi to pick me up there. I had now walked 2.7 miles, all inside the hospital complex.

On occasions when I needed infusions, I had to go to hospital Admissions and fill out paperwork because the infusion was done by the hospital instead of my oncologist's staff. On one of those occasions, I walked across the lobby to Walgreens to pick up a prescription. A young man asked me "What is that book you're reading?" I showed him the cover of "Bible Doctrine" by Wayne Grudem and explained that I was reading it for my current seminary class. He asked, "What's it about?" We proceeded to have a lively conversation about God, the Bible and the Trinity. He bombarded me with a lot of questions. It was both intimidating and fun. If I hadn't been in the process of readmission into the hospital, I never would have met this young man and been able to share my faith. I believe God puts people in our path for a reason. I made some mental notes to do some more research on some of the questions he had asked that I didn't feel I had answered very well.

GVHD

Graft-versus-host disease (GVHD) is a syndrome characterized by inflammation that can occur in different organs. It is commonly associated with bone marrow and stem cell transplants. White blood cells of the donor's immune system that remain in the donated stem cells (the graft) see the recipient (the host) as foreign. The white blood cells in the transplanted tissue attack the recipient's body cells. (Wikipedia) My new immune system was growing and developing well, my doctors said. It was fighting some GVHD, but things were better than expected and my kidney, liver, and other major organ functions were good. My medications were adjusted slightly, and I would be going back every Tuesday and Friday for the next couple of months for the same monitoring regimen. Now back to another seminary paper that was due soon.

January 24 was a good day. I didn't have any lab or doctor appointments. The hotel breakfast was always good, and the staff were always pleasant. I finished my paper for my last seminary class, got it emailed, and Amazon delivered the book for our next class, which would begin February 4. I was venturing outside by myself a little and drove to Walmart for another grocery pickup at the store a few miles from our hotel. It was very nice to back into the parking spot and open the back hatch so the employees could load the groceries into the car.

My leg was healing ever so slowly. We had an appointment with the vascular surgeon the next day. Everything had to be balanced, and results were often like a domino effect. If we backed off certain medications to help my leg heal, we would have to increase other medications, which could cause new problems, and on and on. Patience was key. We continued to lean into God.

January 25. Up at 6:00am, I made coffee and checked my vital signs. My blood pressure, heart rate, and temperature were all good. My blood sugar was lower than recent levels. I spent the morning mostly reading. At my appointment with the vascular surgeon who did my leg surgery, he unwrapped my leg, examined the incision, and squeezed the muscles to see how the tissues were responding. He wrapped my leg from the ankle to the knee to control swelling and said, "looking good – I need to see you in 60 days to do a doppler test for follow up." A doppler test is an ultrasound exam that uses high frequency sound waves to measure blood flow. I asked what his instructions were going forward, and he said, "use it or lose it." Those were clear enough instructions for me. Thank you, God, for getting me over one more obstacle.

That night my GI tract started hurting and acting up. It turned out we couldn't fight the GVHD with oral medications alone. The next morning, I was readmitted to the ICU and received several infusions for rehydration and to tackle the GVHD head on. I had developed diarrhea, one of the conditions that was the most concerning to the doctors and nurses. It continued all day and that night. I had no control over it, and I quickly lost weight and strength. At one point, I was on my hands and knees in the bathroom floor. I didn't have the strength to stand up. I thought I was going to die. I remember praying out loud, "God, please don't let me die like this."

If you ever get in a similar situation, don't give up! I continued to receive IV infusions of fluids, my blood was analyzed regularly, and the nurses were taking good care of me. The diarrhea eventually stopped. Answered prayer. The nurses said I had to get better because they wanted to put me on the payroll so I would continue to get up early and make coffee. Saturday, my doctor said my situation didn't look like GVHD, but we couldn't be too careful, considering my symptoms. He said I would be there overnight again, and he would decide Sunday if we should do another colonoscopy with biopsy. I watched Stonewater church services online and the football games from my hospital room.

Sunday was 30 days since my bone marrow transplant and a big deal as far as I was concerned. Even though I was back in the ICU, I was confident it was only temporary. There were some patients who didn't make this milestone. When I was getting coffee one morning, I met the wife of a transplant patient who was also back in the hospital due to complications he had developed. We talked about similarities in my situation and his. She just broke down in tears because her husband was mad about how things were going, and he was mad at God. I shared how I wasn't mad at God because I had decided from the beginning He was in control, and how that had given me so much peace. I offered to go visit her husband if he would let me, and we prayed together for him. I didn't get to visit with him. I was so grateful for the guidance and love of our God, and the constant flow of prayers to Him from my Stonewater church family, my Fountain Village neighbors, and friends and family members from all over the country. The doctors and nurses at the hospital were amazing. God bless them all.

Debbi came to the hospital, and we were able to watch part of some football games together. I went to sleep right after the second game and my nurse woke me at 10:30pm to begin five infusions of blood, platelets, and electrolytes. The nurse stayed in the room, monitored vital signs, the infusion rates and took blood samples every two hours for lab analysis. I was exhausted Monday morning due to no sleep; therefore, I was going to try to catch up. My doctor had put the biopsy he previously ordered on hold. If one was done, he wanted a full colonoscopy of both upper and lower GI, which would be done on Wednesday. Plans changed again. After more study of my blood work, my doctors wanted to do a photopheresis, which is a procedure that separates blood components. We were waiting to get on the schedule for this amazing machine. Debbi walked the hallway with me that afternoon. A nurse stopped us and said my doctor wanted my current weight. Scales in the hallway showed I weighed 174 pounds in my boxers. I had lost 31 pounds.

That night I slept well and caught up on my sleep. I felt so much better the next morning. By 10:00am I was already walking laps in the hallway. At 2:30pm my nurse found me walking again, scooped me up into a wheelchair and said, "short notice – you are going to photopheresis." Photopheresis is a procedure where blood is drawn from a patient's body, pumped through a machine that separates white blood cells and platelets, treats them with a specialty chemical, exposes them to ultraviolet light, and returns them to the patient's body. The process enhances the performance of the immune system. The procedure took about three hours, was totally painless, and I would go back the next day for the second half of the treatment. Debbi was back in Granbury. I walked 1.3 miles that day.

January 31 marked 34 days since my transplant. I had spent all but seven of them in the hospital. I had the second photopheresis treatment that day, and lab analysis revealed there was now a virus in my blood. As always, the doctors and nurses were right on it. My condition improved dramatically that day and I was discharged from the hospital late that afternoon. Debbi had brought more things from Granbury, and we were back together in our hotel "home away from home". We were both exhausted but got to sleep in the same bed with no scheduled wake ups that night. We were looking forward to doing some online grocery shopping and getting into a healthy eating and exercise routine to keep me out of the hospital. I had lost 33 pounds, so we had some work to do. I never doubted God was going to get us through this.

The next day we had breakfast at the hotel and Debbi drove us to pick up groceries we had ordered online (I was under "no driving" orders). I had a good nap that afternoon and I walked the hotel hallways some. We were getting back on schedule with my medications and insulin routine. Debbi made spaghetti for supper, and we played Scrabble that night.

The next Saturday, our friends Steve and Joni Berry came to Dallas to watch their granddaughter play volleyball, and they came by the hotel for a wonderful visit afterwards. Debbi cooked supper in the Crockpot. Amazon delivered a copy of the new book *Road to Bethel* written by our dear friend Tricia Bullard, and we began reading it together on the sofa. Life was good. God is good.

Sunday morning, we watched the Stonewater church service online, I walked a little, and we had lunch in our room. Debbi watched a movie while I read. In the evening, I went on another long walk. Pastor Joey

White called to check on me, which was very special. I just cannot emphasize how much our Stonewater family meant to us. I signed in and attended my seminary class remotely, and we read a few more chapters of *Road to Bethel* together before going to bed.

Monday morning started with another photopheresis treatment at 8:30am, then to Walgreens in the hospital complex and Debbi picked me up to go back to the hotel. I walked and napped, attended seminary class online, and Debbi cooked a delicious roast for supper. We finished reading *Road to Bethel*. What a life story of faith! Get your hands on a copy. Tricia is an inspiration.

Walking more each day had become a new to-do item. The next day I drove myself to the hospital so Debbi could sleep in, and I intentionally parked in the building D parking garage and walked to building A for my fourth photopheresis treatment at 8:30am. After the treatment, I walked back to building D for blood analysis and meeting with my case manager. She said she was impressed with my progress. I would continue to have different treatments to target GVHD, but my body was cooperating well, and I no longer needed infusions. What an answer to prayer. I walked back to the parking garage and drove to the hotel, took a nap, and walked a little more. Sounds like a lot of walking, but my total was only 1.8 miles. Slow and steady.

In early February, I weighed 172 pounds. I had now lost 33 pounds. Granted, I was a little overweight at the beginning, but I had lost a lot of muscle. Some of my medications were artificially causing high glucose levels, forcing me to take insulin shots several times each day. So, I was on a quest to find recipes we could cook on the stove or in the crockpot that were heart healthy, diabetic-friendly, and high protein.

In addition to my medical issues, we had other challenges. On one of our quick trips to Granbury, Debbi hit a transformer in our neighborhood and knocked out the power to several of our neighbors' homes. The utility company had power restored within a few hours. The GEICO adjuster met us as soon as we returned to the hotel. The car was drivable, but there was quite a bit of damage. He gave us the repair estimate, and we located a nearby body shop. A rental car was included in our coverage, so all was good. We had an appointment to take the car to a dealership the next morning, and the rental car was delivered to the dealership.

On February 9, I reported to the hospital at 1:30pm, blood was taken for analysis, the dressing was changed on my tri-fusion port, and I was prepared for a bone marrow biopsy. Unfortunately, the fibrosis in my bone marrow was so extensive that after three attempts it was determined a sample could not be obtained. A sample of bone marrow was needed to determine if I had any trace of the DNA mutations that caused my cancer. They did get a good piece of actual bone, which would hopefully reveal the information needed. I had no pain during the biopsies, which was a blessing. All my blood readings were good, so all I needed was an hour of IV fluids. With each new challenge, I would search my Bible for scripture that spoke to that challenge. The scripture I felt applied to the day's events was:

"Be anxious for nothing, but in everything by prayer and supplication, with thanksgiving, let your requests be made known by God; and the peace of God, which surpasses all understanding, will guard your hearts and minds through Christ Jesus." Philippians 4:6-7, NKJV

One day I received a hiking merit badge in the mail from my very dear friend Steve Wenger, who I'd known for over 40 years. I could write volumes about memories we had made together on motorcycle trips and phone conversations we had almost weekly over those 40 years. Steve had been following my daily updates and encouraging me to walk and was proud of my progress. The merit badge was a special gift from a very special friend and brother in Christ. My sister Phyllis made a pin for the back of it, and I pinned it to my jacket I wore when I went on my walks.

Superbowl Sunday was cloudy, rainy and kept us inside most of the day. I managed to walk over two miles in the hallways. Debbi made a delicious taco soup in the Crockpot, and we joined half the U.S. population to watch the Super Bowl. While we were watching the game, cheering for our team, and hoping we had that winning square at

Warren' Backyard, we took a minute to be thankful we live in a country with so much freedom!

All my medical information was available through the patient portal. I received an email each time new results were added to the records or I had a message from my medical team. Sunday night I got my bone biopsy results that confirmed I had a blood virus. At 10:00am the next morning my case manager called and said I needed to be back in the hospital to treat the virus because it was "serious". I was re-admitted and soon back in transplant ICU, this time on the 12th floor. The virus I now had attacks primarily the bladder and kidneys. The doctors and nurses were all hands on deck treating me for it. This too, would pass. It was a beautiful day outside. I was getting excellent care. Debbi and I had so many people praying for us.

GVHD episodes are always part of the post-transplant life. They are never a surprise to the doctors I had. They are disappointing, but I didn't see them as setbacks so much as steps I had to take to get where I was going. The virus I now had only occurs in about one out of every 100 transplants. Me, the overachiever again. The "irrigation" of my bladder continued, to address the virus. My doctor was happy with my body's response to the virus treatments. He ordered a blood infusion to increase my hematocrit level and a platelet infusion that night. I would go for another photopheresis treatment the next morning.

After my platelet infusion, tests indicated I no longer needed the blood transfusion because my hematocrit level had increased. I received my photopheresis treatment at 8:30am, was back in my room by 11:30, and my catheter was removed. The virus had been dealt with. Hallelujah.

February 16 was a busy day of tests and treatments. I got a platelets infusion and a blood transfusion so my levels would be high enough to do the next photopheresis treatment. The GVHD treatment doses were changed, my insulin regimen was increased, and two new medications were added to those I was taking at the hotel. I would have an IV chemotherapy treatment that night and would be discharged the next morning.

"My brethren, count it all joy when you fall into various trials, know that the testing of your faith produces patience. But let patience have its perfect work that you may be perfect and complete, lacking nothing." James 1:2-4, NKJV

By this time, I was really beginning to get it. God continued to test me. He continued to give me trials to strengthen my faith. Each time I overcame another hurdle, I was even more enthusiastic about sharing the victory and giving God the glory.

February 17, I had a blood analysis, a platelets infusion, a blood transfusion, and one more chemotherapy treatment. I was discharged from the hospital that afternoon. Debbi got back from Granbury about 30 minutes before all the paperwork was done – great timing! All the chemotherapy and other treatments, plus lying in the hospital bed almost constantly had drained me of energy. I was again dependent on my walker for balance. But I was determined to walk and begin regaining my strength. I was sure looking forward to sleeping with my wife in a normal bed. Sunday morning began my new routine, which was to take three pills on an empty stomach, check my vital signs and blood glucose, give myself two insulin shots, and then eat breakfast within 15 minutes of the second shot. After breakfast, I took 12 more pills, including anti-viral, anti-fungal, and anti-rejection medications. While I was taking my meds, I got an email bill from the hotel for our stay through that day, which is what our original reservation was for. We had originally hoped I would be in the hospital for a couple of weeks after my transplant, then a week or so in the hotel, and then we'd go home to Granbury. With mixed emotions, I called the front desk and extended our reservation for another 30 days, knowing I was scheduled for lab infusions on Mondays, Wednesdays, and Fridays now. Waiting was near torture.

The sun was shining, the sky was clear, and we had so many things to be grateful for. Monday, February 19 was my first scheduled infusion treatment to fight the BK virus, which was now the biggest threat to my body. The BK virus, also called polyomavirus, is a virus that most people get in childhood. Once you get a BK virus infection, the virus stays in your system for good. But it does not cause a problem for most people. This is called *latent*, or like being 'asleep' in your body. Sometimes, when your immune system is not working well, the virus wakes up. It can be life-threatening to transplant patients with compromised immune systems. That's why we were doubling up with infusions three times per week. I would go to the infusion floor and sit in a recliner while IV bag contents were pumped into me. Debbi wanted to come along and see the process until we found out it takes five hours, so she went back to the hotel to wait for me. I had these treatments until favorable results were obtained. I brought my seminary books and Bible with me to future treatments. The good news was that I was being tapered off the steroids, dramatically lowering my blood glucose levels and insulin doses. And my kidney and liver functions remained excellent.

Cancer Free

Three DNA mutations were what caused my cancer in the first place. It had now been two months since we first checked in at the hospital for my transplant. Results from the recent bone marrow biopsy had detected NO mutations in my new bone marrow, and "no diagnostic evidence of a myeloid neoplasm." That meant there were no more cancer-causing cells like those in my original bone marrow and I was cancer free. Praise God!

GERMS! Following this good news, my doctor gave me a stern warning that my new bone marrow was like a newborn baby's. I must avoid as much exposure to germs as possible. NO travel in public places except to and from the hospital. NO exposure to dogs or cats. NO eating fast food or any other outside food because of possible contamination. NO, NO, NO seemed to be the theme. But it was what we had to do to avoid germs and possible infection. We were still on a positive path to a successful transplant outcome. Debbi was going to Granbury for the weekend, to cook beef stew, meatloaf, and other goodies for me to eat while she was away. We had Blue Bell ice cream in the freezer, and a bunch of Joni Berry oatmeal raisin cookies. Those were bound to be good for healing. As always, we were overwhelmed by everyone's care and prayers.

On Friday, February 23, Debbi dropped me off at the hospital at 7:00am. In the elevator, I met a Pastor who volunteers and was on his way to pray for patients who were willing to visit with him. This is something I thought I might like to do some day. It was another long day of lying in hospital beds and getting photopheresis for three hours, then the five-hour treatment I had three days each week. Debbi picked up our car from the body shop before heading home to Granbury and said it looked great. Another step towards normal. My sister Phyllis picked me up at the hospital and took me to the hotel, and boy was I looking forward to a weekend of no hospital appointments!

Saturday, I managed to take my walker and go outside for a walk in the parking lot. I took two naps to catch up on my sleep and read my Bible and seminary book and watched a couple of episodes of "Diners, Drive-Ins, and Dives", one of my favorite TV shows.

Sunday was another beautiful day outside. Another gift from God. My days began at 6:00am, with prayers and coffee, then checking my blood sugar and giving myself insulin shots. The good news was that my blood pressure, heart rate, temperature, and blood sugar were all within normal ranges. The treatments appeared to be working, and the doctors had begun reducing some of my medications. Thank you, Lord. On weekdays I would get ready to go for treatments. But on this morning, I went to the hotel breakfast buffet since there was no crowd, fixed myself a plate and took it back to the room. I just couldn't resist the biscuits and sausage gravy! I watched the Stonewater Church service online, walked 1.5 miles, studied for my seminary class, and took an afternoon nap. Debbi got back from Granbury with meatloaf for supper – YUM.

February 26. There was a beautiful sunrise that morning. Debbi dropped me off at the hospital for lab work and a five-hour infusion. My lab results kept improving. I was able to read my Bible and talk on the phone with a couple of old friends during the treatments. With treatments taking up three days a week, I really appreciated Tuesdays and Thursdays off. I still had a strict schedule for taking medications and eating meals, but I was at the hotel and not in the hospital. Debbi and I had breakfast together, took short walks around the parking lot, and we both took naps. I joined a corporate sponsored program called GVHD Speaks, which includes several ways for people with GVHD to share their stories with others through different forms of media and mentoring. This was a way for me to share my faith with many people.

The last day of February, I met my walking goal of 1.8 miles, and I was able to safely walk short distances without my walker. Steady progress. Some of the trees were already beginning to bloom; signs that spring was approaching. When I arrived at the hospital for my 8:00am photopheresis treatment, I was told my treatments had been reduced from twice weekly to twice every other week, and my five-hour cidofovir treatments were being reduced from three days per week to two days per week. The nurses apologized because they were unable to notify me ahead of time and gave me the new photopheresis appointment dates for March. I could have been upset about showing up for nothing but praised God instead. We were all smiling. The struggle continued, and my treatment regimen was inconvenient and frustrating sometimes, but I had never been in pain for any length of time. I had never had nausea or other nasty side effects from the chemotherapy, and every single day I had an opportunity to say "Good morning" with a smile and possibly share my faith. I didn't make my walking goal that day (too many hours in treatments) but I did make 1.8 miles.

It was hard to believe we'd been temporarily living in Dallas since before Christmas. I had labs, met with my case manager, and another five-hour treatment beginning at 8:30am. Since I didn't have any treatments scheduled for Monday, we were looking forward to spending a long weekend at home in Granbury. In the meeting with my case manager, she was excited to tell me the latest analysis of my bone marrow showed the donor stem cells were producing new blood cells that matched my previous blood 100%. This was HUGE. I was literally in tears. Our God was victorious. I would continue to have the photopheresis and cidofovir chemotherapy infusions and would have blood work done weekly until my blood cell counts were within normal ranges. We were on a positive trajectory toward that goal.

March 2. What a nice day we had in Granbury that day. Debbi went to the grocery store and got some things for the weekend, and I made three dozen of her favorite cookies – pecan sandies. The high temperature for the day was 86 degrees, with sunshine all day. I rode my three-wheel motorcycle to the gas station and Kroger and ran into our neighbor Sue White and our Stonewater paster Beau Mills in the parking lot. It was so nice to be outside and see friends. Riding my motorcycle, even if only a few miles, was a huge pleasure. Steve and Joni

Berry were hosting a book signing celebration at Warren's Backyard for our dear friend Tricia Bullard, author of *"Road to Bethel"*. Knowing I was trying to avoid crowds, Steve invited me to come to the back door where he would have slices of cake for me and Debbi. I had intended to grab the cake and run but was able to shake hands with Tricia and get a signed copy of her book. So many of our church family and friends came over to say hello, this being the first time we had seen each other in nearly six months. We used masks and hand sanitizer, and I thanked all for taking precautions and for their continued prayers. I grilled steaks that evening, which were a hit. Debbi loves steaks grilled outside, and the dogs love the T-bones. Sadly, not many things tasted normal to me because the chemotherapy had affected my taste buds. Hopefully, it wasn't permanent. Fortunately, I had a good appetite. Next trip home, I planned to put a brisket on the smoker.

Monday morning, I was up early, made coffee, checked my vital signs, took my insulin shots and morning medications, and ate breakfast. I had a mid-morning nap, lunch, and we drove back to Dallas to the hotel. It was so nice to have an extended weekend in Granbury and see friends and neighbors. Debbi dropped me off at the hospital Tuesday morning. My son Adam texted me from Denver and said employees at the coffee shop asked about me. Friends of his in Denver were asking about me! It was overwhelming how many people cared and kept up with my condition. I was so grateful for them all. The weather was so nice that I decided to try and walk (with my walker) from the hospital to the hotel. There was a hike and bike trail along Park Central Boulevard with benches where I could stop and rest, which I did about a dozen times. But I made it – 1.3 miles. Wednesday, I didn't have any doctor appointments or treatments, so I was able to run some errands, take naps, and do a lot of reading. I finished and turned in my seminary paper for the last class and started working on our income taxes. The IRS doesn't care if you're having medical issues, and that April 15 deadline was quickly approaching. I would much rather have been reading about Matthew the tax collector than doing our taxes.

Thursday, I had a photopheresis treatment at 8:00am and I thought I'd go home by 11:30. But my lab work indicated I needed a platelet infusion AND two units of blood before the photopheresis could be done. So, the actual treatment wasn't complete until after 5:00pm. Lying in the hospital bed all day Tuesday and Thursday sure reminded me how fortunate I was to NOT be in the hospital full time! Friday, I was in photopheresis at 7:00am getting an early start because my five-hour infusion was scheduled for later that morning. Well, the best laid plans didn't materialize. My labs showed I was low on several blood components, so I had to have another blood transfusion, which added an hour to the day. Prior to my five-hour treatment, the analysis showed a chemo component elevated, so I had to do more labs with blood drawn from a traditional IV needle in my arm instead of my ports. Another hour added to the day. Finally, my chemo started at 1:00pm and was completed at 6:00. None of this was bad news; it just happens. The good news was that we were still making gradual progress, and we were able to go home to Granbury nearly every weekend. Saturday, I baked another four dozen pecan sandies and gave most of them away to neighbors who were caring for our dogs, checking our mail, and who were praying for me. I loved sharing the cookies, and pecan sandies were a good "thank you" gift. I planned to bake and give away a lot more of them.

A study by the National Institutes of Health in Washington, D.C. concluded that 20-40% of all cancer patients die from causes related to malnutrition. One of the things I was dealing with now was the loss of taste. When I grilled steaks the last weekend, Debbi loved hers, but I couldn't taste mine. In fact, any beef I had tried recently just didn't taste like it was supposed to. Chicken still tasted the same, Blue Bell ice cream tasted the same, and coffee tasted the same (praise the Lord). I needed protein, and my medications included magnesium three times a day, but I was concentrating on identifying foods that were both good for me AND tasted good. Eggs and bacon still tasted good (thank you, God!). Debbi understood and was helping as much as she could. The good news? I like fruits and vegetables, and I had gained four pounds – I was up to 176 now. Patience, perseverance, and trust.

"rejoicing in hope, patient in tribulation, continuing steadfastly in prayer." Romans 12:12, NKJV

We started to venture out to restaurants, being cautious about exposure to other people. We went to a little Mexican food café we like near our house, waiting until 2:00pm so there wasn't a crowd, and we were in a booth separated a good distance from other diners. It was nice eating out again together. The cheese enchiladas, beans, and rice all tasted good, so they went on the list of things to eat often. For supper, we went to Wings & More in Granbury. Our server introduced himself as Isaac. I asked him to keep his distance and told him why, which he completely understood. I told him I liked his Biblical name, and he said all his siblings also had Biblical names. And we found out he goes to Stonewater church. He was an excellent server, listened well, and earned a good tip. The wings tasted great – interesting how beef no longer tasted good at all, but chicken did.

March 10. What a beautiful day! One of my projects for the day was to replace the battery in my Moto Guzzi motorcycle to get it ready to sell. Sitting dormant through the cold winter, even in the garage just killed the battery. I had to go to three auto parts stores to find the right replacement battery. The bike started right up and ran well. I had a new set of motorcycle tires I sold back in September of last year, but the buyer, a friend named Clayton hadn't come to pick them up due to me being in the hospital for my transplant and it being winter. He drove down and picked up the tires and we had a good visit, AND he bought the Moto Guzzi! He came back a couple of weeks later and picked it up. While at breakfast, Clayton shared an analogy. He asked if we had ever watched how a contestant in a stock show keeps their pig walking in a straight line in front of the judges? They walk behind their pig and use a thin fiberglass rod about six feet long, gently tapping the pig on the left or right, depending on which direction the pig is going off course. Clayton compared this technique to how the Holy Spirit encourages us to walk. I will never forget the comparison.

Monday was another beautiful day, with sunshine, blue skies, good coffee, and a day with my bride. I felt like the Holy Spirit was telling me to write about how my faith had been so important during my transplant journey. I had taken some notes and written down some ideas. Tricia Bullard was kind enough to share a transcript template used by some authors. So, I officially started this book.

Tuesday morning, I was up early again, made coffee, read some in the book of Acts, then checked my vitals, which were all good numbers to start the day. Later, at the hospital, I had blood work done, COVID swabs, a five-hour Cidofovir infusion, then a platelet infusion. The reason for the COVID swab was because of my loss of taste – just precautionary. It was a long day, but one more day of healing. We hear often how Jesus told the disciples to "witness to the ends of the earth." This is the Great Commission. But we don't often remember that Jesus also told them to wait, until they were baptized with the Holy Spirit. He also told them

"It is not for you to know times or seasons which the Father has put in His own authority." Acts 1:7, NKJV

Debbi and I had reminded ourselves repeatedly that it was futile to try and predict when my treatments would be over – only God knows.

Wednesday was laid back. I got up early to check my vitals and take meds, have a cup of coffee and read some more of Acts. I lied down on the sofa and fell asleep for another two hours. We went to Barnes & Noble and bought a couple of books and I did some research on self-publishing and started putting some thoughts in writing on the template Tricia shared with me. For supper, we went to Fish City Grill to see if my taste buds would recognize fish. I ordered blackened trout (without all the seasoning), rice, and blanched spinach. It ALL tasted good. Even the key lime pie tasted normal. Woohoo! A bonus was that fish is nutritious – and so is key lime pie, I'm pretty sure. A nice supper date.

March 14. It was nice to have weeks like this one where I had treatments on Tuesdays and Fridays, with three days off. We hung around the hotel until noon, picked up prescription refills at the pharmacy and went to Macy's. I bought some pants that were two inches smaller in the waist and shorter in length. I was still down over 40 pounds from what I weighed before my transplant and my pants were just not fitting any more. We had leftover chicken spaghetti for supper, and we settled in for the evening, hoping the thunderstorms in the area would continue to go north of us. On Friday, we got good news, not-so-good news, and good news. First thing in the morning, I woke up and opened my gift of another day. The Holy Spirit was already up and waiting on me. I swung my legs out of the bed and walked under my own power to the coffee pot. There were people living under the freeway overpasses less than 100 yards from our hotel. I thanked the Lord for my warm bed and dry hotel room. The not-so-good news included a notice from my insurance company that my January medical costs were $38,562. Plus, prescription costs were $18,124. The good news – our cost was $4,539. That was a lot of money for one month, but some of those prescriptions would last 90 days. I was already off a couple of them and taking fewer of others. Instead of panicking, we were grateful I had such good insurance coverage. Back at the hospital, my lab results showed increased white blood cell, red blood cell, and platelets counts. All were good improvements. I took my laptop with me to help keep me occupied while I sat for six hours of infusions.

Saturday, it rained most of the day, so it was a good day to stay inside and bake cookies. I drove to the bank, and on the way back and dropped off some cookies to some of my prayer warriors in our neighborhood. Later that evening, we dropped off some more when we walked the dogs. We so much appreciated people who had been praying for months. Rick and Ann Frye dropped off supper and visited for a while. They really knocked it out of the park with the pork tenderloin Rick grilled, and Ann made squash, baked sweet potatoes, bread, and dessert. Sunday, I baked another two dozen cookies and ended up giving away six dozen that weekend. It was nice to spend another weekend at home.

Monday, March 19 was three months since I was admitted into the hospital. I had my next-to-last photopheresis treatment that morning, and for the first time I didn't need a blood transfusion before the treatment. We were still dealing with the BK virus, but signs continued to indicate we were making good progress on that as well. That Friday,

I had my last photopheresis treatment, which started at 7:30am and was done by noon, I was out of my 5-hr cidofovir infusion by 3:00pm and we were home in Granbury before dark.

Saturday, we met for breakfast with the buyers of the Moto Guzzi. They came to the house and loaded it up for the trip to its new home in Oklahoma. I was sad to see it leave, but happy for the new owners. They were a couple we could see ourselves being longtime friends with, and promised to come visit them and see their ranch.

The following is from a book I was reading at the time titled *The Seven Longest Yards*: "For most of my life, Jesus sat on the bench like a pitch hitter. He was ready to take the field in case disaster struck, but He wasn't on the roster. I only prayed when I really needed help, but most of the time I tried to handle whatever life threw at me on my own. God wasn't a priority, and He certainly wasn't part of my day-to-day life unless I was desperate." How many of us have been there or know someone who was? I am so grateful for the personal relationship I have with Jesus and the daily friendship I have with the Holy Spirit. *The Seven Longest Yards*, by Chris and Emily Norton is about a college football player who broke his neck during a game and became a quadriplegic, being told he would never walk again. It is the story of how he and his fiancé' Emily overcame obstacles and how they leaned on their faith and each other. I recommend it.

The next Tuesday, my iPhone's facial recognition didn't recognize my face. An indication of how much weight I'd lost. Debbi stayed in Granbury for a doctor appointment, and to work in her flowerbeds, which she loves to do. On the trip back to Dallas, I took Hwy 4 from Acton to Cleburne, then Hwy 67 to Dallas. I got to see lots of beautiful bluebonnets and much less traffic. I met my sister Phyllis in Plano for supper and a visit. Sadly, there were notices on the restaurant doors announcing the closing in April. So many customers would be saddened by the loss of an endeared place where they had eaten for decades, and so many employees would lose their jobs. I prayed they would be able to recover quickly.

Wednesday was a good day. My doctor reduced my steroid dosage to 2.5mg compared to 80mg two months prior. As a result, my blood sugar had gone down, and I was able to take fewer units of insulin. I didn't have any appointments, so I was able to relax, read, and walk around the parking lot to get some steps in. I was feeling a little sorry for myself and impatient with my slow recovery, then I read again:

"Be anxious for nothing, but in everything by prayer and supplication, with thanksgiving, let your requests be made known to God; and the peace of God, which surpasses all understanding, will guard your hearts and minds through Christ Jesus." Philippians 4:6-7, NKJV

Amazing how the Holy Spirit guides us back on track.

Thursday, I had an appointment with the vascular surgeon who removed the clot from my left leg back in December. They did a doppler test to see how the circulation was in that leg. The results were very good. The swelling in the leg was from fluid retention, not a circulation problem. My primary care doctor had prescribed a medication to address fluid retention just the past Tuesday. It was encouraging that the diagnosis from both doctors was the same. In the meantime, I would wear a compression sleeve and give the new medication time to work.

Friday was another long day of lab work and infusions in two different buildings that started at 8:30am and ended at 6:30pm, including picking up more prescriptions at the pharmacies. All small accomplishments compared to the real significance of Good Friday. I vividly remember attending a church several years ago where the pastor ended his sermon with the statement, "We can choose to live in the darkness of Friday or the light of Sunday." It reminded me how the darkest day in history resulted in the brightest future possible being available to anyone who will believe with their heart that Jesus is our living Savior. Every time someone said, "Happy Friday" I replied, "Happy Good Friday." I had some very good discussions with several nurses about faith and forgiveness that day.

Coincidence: a remarkable occurrence of events or circumstances without apparent causal connection (according to a popular dictionary).

The past few days, I had been a little down because we couldn't attend Easter Sunday services, and my condition wasn't improving as quickly as we would like it to. In fact, I now had a new development of GVHD causing ulcers on my tongue and in my mouth that were very painful. A good friend and fellow Stonewater church member shared a daily devotional with me every morning. Was it coincidence that morning's message focused on suffering?

> "Therefore, having been justified by faith, we have peace with God through our Lord Jesus Christ, through whom also we have access by faith into this grace in which we stand, and rejoice in hope of the glory of God. And not only that, but we also glory in tribulations, knowing that tribulation produces perseverance; and perseverance, character; and character, hope." Romans 5:1-4, NKJV

Was it coincidence when I opened my Bible that morning to continue reading Acts, I soon came upon scripture about Paul being repeatedly beaten and thrown in prison? Was it coincidence that a friend's Facebook post was about the repeated sufferings of Job? I don't think any were coincidence. I believe the Holy Spirit was reminding me that my pains were small compared to some that others have endured. I was grateful for the reminders. God is good all the time.

My infusion went well on Tuesday and there were some slight improvements in my blood test results. I was still low on magnesium, so that was added as a second infusion. Wednesday night I woke up with an attack of gout in my right foot. I had had gout twice before, the latest about ten years earlier. I called my doctor's office, and they called in a prescription to address it.

Thursday the weather was beautiful. We went by the hospital and picked up prescriptions, went by the Verizon store to work out some issues with my phone, and spent the afternoon driving around different neighborhoods in nearby small towns. All these towns had been mostly ranches and farmland and were now dominated by huge, beautiful

71

homes, many on one-acre lots. We drove by South Fork Ranch, which Debbi had never seen in person. We stopped at Olive Garden for an early supper, where Debbi had soup and salad, and I was able to eat soup and fettuccine Alfredo despite the sores in my mouth. The gout in my right foot was very painful, but I was happier being outside than just lying in bed or sitting on the couch in the hotel room. I would be sitting all day the next day during more infusions. While driving, we saw homeless people living under bridges and begging for money at intersections. We saw one man walking in a highway lane waving his arms and yelling as if he was having a heated argument with someone... maybe demons from malnutrition, or drug abuse, or PTSD. I prayed those people would find help and comfort and come to know Jesus. I thanked our Lord for reminding me that my troubles are quite minor compared to those of some others.

On April 5 we got the good news that several of my blood readings had improved, and my care team was reducing some more of the medications I had been taking. Medications designed to specifically treat the sores in my mouth were prescribed. It was a long day of infusions, but the trip to Granbury that evening was uneventful – beautiful weather and all the other drivers stayed in their lanes.

Saturday, it was nice to be back home for the weekend. We donned our masks, rented a U-Haul truck and picked up a hutch/bookcase we had bought at the Bella Rosa consignment shop. When we were dollying it out to the truck, two men offered to help, and they were VERY helpful. I asked where they go to church, and one said First Baptist and the other said Stonewater. We unloaded the hutch at home and returned the U-Haul truck. I really enjoyed moving my books from my desk and closet into organized groups in the new hutch. On top went the Lego tractor Adam gave me to assemble while I was in the transplant ICU.

Adam and his friend Cordelia flew in from Denver to watch the lunar eclipse. They flew in a few days early because Cordelia had never been to Texas, and he showed her around the city. We had planned to drive south of Granbury and find a good vantage point for watching the eclipse. Instead, we were invited to an eclipse-watching "pasture party" and had a wonderful time. The picnic menu included "Moon

Pies" for dessert – very clever! It was so kind of Danny and Kathleen for hosting and so wonderful to see so many special friends that day. We had dinner that night and shared a free tiramisu with a single candle in it to celebrate my birthday. It would be my #1 birthday since my bone marrow transplant. I was so grateful for the generosity of the donor, the doctors, the nurses, the technology, the medications that had saved my life, for all who had prayed for me and Debbi, and to God for providing and orchestrating the entire process.

April 9 was a great 71st birthday. Adam and Cordelia came over for birthday cake, and to sing and celebrate. I got cards, phone calls and so many good wishes via Facebook, texts, and emails!

The next day we were back in Dallas for more infusions. I always had blood taken for lab analysis first, then a meeting with my case manager, and then the 5-hour infusions. In our meeting, my case manager said my blood work was continuing to slowly improve. I was now being completely taken off one of the steroids. Another pill I had been taking for bacterial infections was also being put on hold. I was so grateful to be taking less medications instead of more. My gout had almost disappeared, and I was able to walk without pain again. Praise God.

Friday was another long day, with lab work first, then the meeting with my case manager. After that, I got an infusion of anti-nausea medicine so I wouldn't get sick during the next infusion of Pentamidine, which is a preventative medication to be sure I didn't get a type of pneumonia common in transplant patients. Then the last two hours was my Cidofovir infusion, which is the one I got every Tuesday and Friday to treat the pesky BK virus. The good news was my white blood count had increased to 4.9 and was in the "normal" range for the first time since my transplant. The magic of chemistry, the incredible omnipotence of our God.

The following Monday, I was happy the gout in my right foot was gone and the mouth sores were almost gone as well. This was a big deal because the mouth sores were a type of GVHD. The next day, it was raining when I got up in Dallas. I went to the hospital at 8:30am for my labs and to meet with my case manager. The only thing she changed was my long-acting insulin from 15 to 10 units per day. My lab results showed a slight decrease in white blood cells, red blood cells, and platelets, but nothing alarming. She did add magnesium to my infusions, which made the day even longer. Then we found out they had over-booked in the infusion center I normally go to, so I had to go to building C. To get there, I had to go out in the rain again and drive to a different parking garage. I was beginning to grumble when I got to the infusion floor, but it was so nice and warm compared to the other one, had much better recliners, and I was greeted with "Hi Mr. Greenwade, we're glad you're here…we've heard about what a nice patient you are." End of grumbling. When I next looked on Facebook, one of my friends had posted the following scripture that states we will have trials, and we must keep the faith.

> "In this you greatly rejoice, though now for a little while, if need be, you have been grieved by various trials, that the genuineness of your faith your faith, being much more precious than gold that perishes, though it has been tested by fire, may be found to praise, honor, and glory at the revelation of Jesus Christ." 1Peter 1:5-7, NKJV

REALLY end of my grumbling. I realized I had a new group of people to witness to. I talked with a lady who was getting chemotherapy for breast cancer, and we shared our stories about our cancers and faith. The rain stopped mid-day, the skies cleared, and the day turned out to be beautiful.

On April 17 I had an appointment with my dermatologist in Fort Worth to check out a rough place near my left temple, and it was NOT skin cancer. Thank you, Lord. While there, he did a full body scan and only found a few spots on my scalp that he recommended freezing with liquid nitrogen as a preventative measure.

April 18 was another busy day. We met with my primary care physician at 8:15am in Fort Worth for my annual Medicare wellness exam, filled her in on my transplant and recovery status. She had a list of things she wanted my transplant doctor to send to her – mostly lab results and clinical notes. I drove to Dallas, unpacked at the hotel and went to my 3:15pm appointment at Mandalay Hearing Aid Center, which is a family-owned business with old-fashioned courtesy, customer service and the latest in products and technology. David Steele gave me a thorough hearing test that showed my hearing loss had not changed since my exam in August of last year. However, my hearing aids were fitted with the wrong size ear canal tips, and they were improperly programmed. He changed the tips, had some spares in stock, and spent a lot of time reprogramming my hearing aids. The improvement was immediately noticeable to me. I hoped Debbi would be able to tell a difference when I got home.

When I got to the infusion center Friday morning, I was the only one there. The nurse took my blood for lab analysis and got my infusions started right away. In 20 minutes, my lab results were back. My WBC was 5.0 – within the 4.8-10.8 range! RBC, HGB, HCT, and platelets were also all up. So exciting! During my infusions, I worked on my book draft and almost completed chapter 2. I drove to Granbury after and was home by dark. I walked 1.9 miles total that day and was looking forward to a weekend at home.

Tuesday morning, my lab results were not what I expected. My WBC took a dive from 5.0 to 2.4 and several other readings also went down. Although disappointing, the numbers were not alarming to my doctor, who said these were normal fluctuations. The mouth sores appeared to be completely gone, so there were three medications I no longer had to take. When I was sitting in the infusion room reviewing my lab results, I looked up and a man came in the room in a wheelchair, both legs amputated right above his ankles. I believe the Holy Spirit was saying "Bill, pray for that man and be grateful." We got a late start on my infusions, so I didn't get done until 4:00pm. I had to pick up refills from the pharmacy and didn't get on the road home until peak rush hour. But it was a blessing in a way, because driving 35mph in DFW traffic is a lot safer than the NASCAR speeds most people normally drive. I was safely home before dark.

Wednesday morning, I had a phone call from GVHD Speaks. The call was very informative and satisfying, knowing that sharing my experience might be encouraging for others. Debbi and I went to Cheyne Eye Center in Granbury, had full eye exams and ordered new glasses. Both of us just needed minor changes to our lenses. I still had no sign of cataracts. That night I attended one of my seminary classes online.

Thursday morning, I rode with my neighbor Tom to the Men's Bible Study at Stonewater. We were all glad to see each other after not being able to attend for over four months. This group of men is so supportive, and we have all become very close. If you have an opportunity to join a small group, please do. Being a member of a small group gives you an opportunity to share your feelings, opinions, and faith with others. Members of a small group can develop close relationships with each other and provide emotional support and accountability. You can laugh together and cry together. My knowledge has grown, and my faith has grown by being involved in our small group.

One day, while I sat in the lobby waiting for the infusion lab to open, I watched a couple checking into the hospital with their suitcases and extra things they would need for an extended stay. That was us on December 20, over four months ago. We were so grateful to God for providing a donor, an excellent hospital, doctors and nurses, and to all our friends and relatives who had prayed for us without ceasing.

Saturday was a lazy day until storms that night. We were kept awake by our dog Bella's panic attacks and our dog Hope's snoring through it all. Sunday, we watched the Stonewater early service online and I watched one of my seminary classes online. Sunday night, we attended the first IMPACT meeting in five months. We were so happy to see our IMPACT family, and to say thank you for praying for us the past five months. Adam Richards did a great job of leading our prayer worship with old hymns.

Tuesday was infusion day. There was no sign of the GVHD mouth sores coming back, thank you God and Dexamethasone. I finished another seminary class online and worked on my book a little.

Friday there were clear skies and sunshine to start the day. I had infusions from 8:30am to 3:00pm. My lab results were not encouraging, and the infusions wore me out. I had a restless night, which was always the case after each day of infusions. I got up early Saturday morning and checked my vital signs and blood sugar, then went back to bed and slept most of the morning. That afternoon, we drove over to Waxahachie to watch our grandson Luke play in his baseball game, and visited with daughter Karen, son-in-law Joel, and grandson Beau. This was the first time we'd seen them since December. God grows grandchildren so quickly, it seems!

Monday morning, I ran some errands, including a stop at the post office to get my passport renewed. When my doctor would allow me to travel and I wouldn't need infusions twice a week, I was planning to take Debbi on some trips where passports might be needed. We hoped our first excursion would be a cruise in October with a group from our church. While out running errands, I felt a sharp pain in my right eye each time I stepped out into the sunshine. Before leaving for Dallas, I stopped by Cheyne Eye Center and they were able to work me into their schedule due to a cancellation. The technician repeated all the tests done a couple of weeks ago for comparison, and the optometrist dilated my right eye to do some more tests. I was diagnosed with a condition called uveitis. I was given eyedrops to use until I could meet with an ophthalmologist the next day. I was praying this was not GVHD.

"Trust in the Lord with all your heart and lean not on your own understanding; In all your ways acknowledge Him, and He shall direct your paths." Proverbs 3:5-6, NKJV

"With all your heart" is difficult, especially when we have been trained to "get 'er done." It took everyday effort for me to give up control and listen to God for guidance. Some of my lab results were better this day, and some were not. My oncologist continued to adjust my medication doses accordingly, and I had to have a blood transfusion after my regular infusion. She also ordered a referral to a specialist for the uveitis in my right eye. The eye drops helped with the pain, but my vision was very blurry in that eye. My last infusion didn't start until after 5:00pm, so I got on the road right in the middle of the rush hour traffic and then got delayed at the Cresson train crossing. I got home at 8:30pm.

Wednesday was a good day. The eye drops had almost eliminated my right eye pain and the gout in my foot seemed to be diminishing. I still could not focus with my right eye. Hopefully, I'd be able to see a specialist soon. That night, Debbi and I enjoyed dinner at Christina's on the square in Granbury with Steve and Joni Berry. I was still having a lot of trouble with loss of taste, but salmon is one of the few things that tasted good, and the Parmesan crusted salmon at Christina's was very good.

Thursday morning, I went to the Bible study group meeting at Stonewater, then finished and turned in my paper for the latest seminary class. The big thunderstorm that came through delayed my trip back to the hotel in Dallas, but late in the day the traffic was light, and the skies were clear.

Friday morning my lab work related to the BK virus had improved enough that I did not need a Cidofovir infusion, so it was a short day. My platelets count was way up, but other counts were down, which might have been due to my immune system fighting the infection in my eye. Sunday night, I received new lab results via the patient portal, and the BK virus "copies per ml" had gone down from 500 million to 129 million. Progress!

Tuesday morning, I was at the hospital at 8:30am to have blood drawn for lab analysis, then met with my oncologist. My WBC had increased from 2.0 to 2.7, my RBC was steady, my platelets were up, and my magnesium was up into the normal range for the first time since my transplant. However, things didn't go well Tuesday night. I was sick at my stomach all night and didn't get any sleep. Wednesday morning, I went to a cancer patient physical therapy facility in Dallas for an evaluation to determine what exercises I could do for my weakness and how to address the swelling in my legs. I would go twice a week for the next six weeks and do a series of exercises, and a machine would compress my legs to force fluid out of the tissues. I was sick all afternoon and was still running a slight fever. Debbi was going with me for my Friday tests and infusions so she could be in on the meeting with my oncologist and to drive if I was still feeling bad. One step forward, two steps back sometimes.

Friday, I had blood work done first thing, then Debbi and I met again with my oncologist. She was happy with my lab results and told us I didn't need to have any infusions that day because my immune system appeared to be winning the battle against the BK virus. Answered prayers! I still had constant stomach pain, so an X-ray was done before we headed home. We were anxious to hear if anything showed up on the X-ray. I would go back to Dallas for physical therapy and Tuesday morning labs, then meet with my oncologist, and have infusions. If nothing showed on the X-ray, then I'd probably have a CT scan or MRI to try and identify the source of my stomach pain. Praise God that I no longer had any known GVHD issues.

Monday, I drove to Dallas for my first PT session, which was concentrated on regaining arm strength. It was a good session, and I came away with very sore arms and a list of exercises to do at home. My Tuesday appointment was at 1:30pm, which was the first time it had been that late in the day. I had blood drawn for labs and my tri-fusion port dressing was changed, then I met with my oncologist. Nothing unusual showed on my X-ray. My stomach issues were likely adjustments to big changes in chemotherapy and medications. The reason my appointment was at 1:30pm was because I no longer needed to have regular infusions. I would only have to go to Dallas for lab work and meetings with my oncologist once per week now. The light at the end of the tunnel appeared to be getting brighter.

Tuesday morning, we were awakened at 5:00am by tornado sirens near the hotel in Dallas. Branches were being ripped from trees and tossed across the parking lots. The wind and heavy rain continued for several hours. Thank God there wasn't any of the reported large hail near us.

I had blood drawn and dressing changed at 10:30am, we met with my oncologist, and my lab reports were good. She reduced the dosage on two of my medications, took me off two more meds completely, and I no longer had to have insulin shots. I would keep checking my blood sugar several times a day, and we would continue labs and meetings every Tuesday – just once per week.

My new immune system was not having to fight anything at the present. The blood cell counts continued to increase slowly but were far from "normal" ranges. So, I still had to be careful about getting a cold, the flu, or any other bugs. I was still having digestion issues, and my legs were swollen from fluid retention. I was going to PT in Dallas once a week and had exercises I was doing at home to build strength and endurance. God had brought me so far!

I had PT early Thursday morning, May 30 so I stayed at the hotel Wednesday night to avoid morning traffic. The parking lot was FULL because of power outages in people's homes and other nearby hotels. I was so grateful our home in Granbury and our hotel were spared during the recent storms. There was no power at the PT facility, but they were still operating for patients who wanted to work out.

I went to my PT session in Dallas Monday afternoon. They still didn't have electricity restored to their building, so it didn't take long to work up a sweat. The exercises were already making a difference in my stamina. Tuesday morning, I had labs done and met with my case manager. My lab results showed my WBC, RBC, hemoglobin, and platelet counts all continued to improve, but my kidney functions indicated that the BK virus might now be affecting my kidneys. I had an infusion of fluids to give my kidneys some help. We would get more lab results Wednesday to see what to do next. Two steps forward, two steps back. I trusted God would reveal our next steps soon.

The first week of June, Debbi and I went on a road trip to South Texas. After my Thursday morning Bible study, we drove from Granbury to Victoria, TX and had supper with friends J.L. and Judy. Judy was very kind to accommodate my unpredictable taste buds, and we had a great visit before going to our hotel for the night. Friday morning, we drove from Victoria to Refugio, and I showed Debbi the home where I grew up and Refugio High School. Refugio played Iowa Park for the 1970 State Championship in 2A football. I was in the Refugio band and Debbi was an Iowa Park cheerleader. We had been on the same football field 54 years ago.

On the way to our next hotel in Rockport, we stopped by Oakwood cemetery south of Refugio to visit the gravesites of my parents. My mother died in January, while I was in the hospital following my transplant, and I was unable to attend her funeral. It was an emotional visit.

Friday afternoon, we drove over to Portland, TX and visited with my cousins Doris and Peter. We went to Corpus Christi for supper at the Water Street Oyster Bar, one of my favorite restaurants. We had a great dinner and visit. Doris's son Keith had received a bone marrow transplant several years ago for leukemia. Keith and I were close to the same age, and we were close cousins growing up. Doris was one of my most faithful prayer warriors.

Saturday morning, we drove around Rockport a little and stopped to watch two shrimpers sorting their catch. There was quite a gathering of gulls and pelicans waiting for scraps! We headed back north, stopping in Beeville for lunch and in Dripping Springs to spend the night. We had supper at Homespun Kitchen and Bar, where the food and service were superb – we highly recommend it. On the way back home Sunday morning, we had brunch in Dripping Springs at Crepes a café named Crepes Crazy, which is owned and managed by women who are deaf. The food was amazing, and the employees were all so kind and gracious. If you are in the area, please stop by and give them your business.

Monday, I was back in Dallas for physical therapy. The session included using two small hand-held devices that I squeezed with my hands and individual fingers, one at a time. I never would have guessed these two little gadgets would exercise so many arm and shoulder muscles! I could already tell PT was improving my upper body strength. My lab results came in about noon. WBC was in the normal range for the first time since my transplant, platelets count was highest since my transplant, ANC was in the normal range, kidney functions were back to normal, so no Cidofovir infusion that day. Answered prayers!

Have you ever had one of those nights when your brain will just not be quiet and let you sleep? I got up at 2:00am, wide awake. I didn't go straight to my phone or computer because they are suspected of contributing to sleeping disorders. I read a book for a while, then started on my "To-Do" list, which is always lengthy. I spent most of the afternoon at the dentist, who was able to do some work we had to postpone for six months due to my low platelets level. My platelets were back in the normal range and my dentist was back in my wallet.

Friday morning, after my routine of medications and PT exercises at home, we went to a nursing and rehabilitation facility in Fort Worth to participate in a "car show' for the residents who were able to come outside the building for a few hours. The plan included parking our cool old classic cars under the patio at the main entrance for the residents to see, and some of the nursing staff made popcorn and snow cones. One man designated himself the event DJ and played music off his iPhone for the group. When Debbi and I got there, we parked our 1987 Jeep pickup right in front, went inside to let the event coordinator know we were there, and waited. No other cars showed up. The car club that originally planned to be there backed out. We were the only vehicle there! We weren't members of that club, and we were SO glad we went. When the residents started coming outside, many with the help of nurses, we introduced ourselves and visited with them. Debbi really "worked the crowd" and got several of them to talk who were reluctant at first. As I approached one woman in a wheelchair, whose name was Melba, she said "Mister, you are one hot cookie!" LOL. I thanked her for the compliment and showed her my wedding ring. She joked about Debbi getting her claws in me first. We had a wonderful visit with her. Another woman named Hazel told us how she got her name from a popular TV show in the 1960's. Debbi and I remembered watching this TV show when we were kids.

All the people we visited with were wheelchair bound. Their ages varied from 53 to over 80. Some could speak, some could not, some could feed themselves and some could not. The majority smiled and talked about their experiences. One man, the DJ, had lost both his feet to frostbite while living homeless on the streets. Another man, Cedric, was recovering from multiple strokes and his son had been murdered while he was hospitalized. Carlos was also recovering from a stroke, lost his job and his apartment. He had been a star athlete in high school. When I asked if he could pick one thing he would like somebody to bring him, he said he would love to have a bucket of Kentucky Fried Chicken, corn on the cob, and mashed potatoes. I think what so many of the residents needed was for someone to just listen.

We talked cars, sports, favorite foods, and about Jesus. I asked Cedric if he had his own Bible, and he said yes. What he needed was a highlighter to mark passages in it. I gave him one I had in the truck. We laughed a lot. At times I had tears in my eyes. When the event was over, the nurses had to almost pry a couple of the residents back inside. We left with joy in our hearts. It was one of the most rewarding days Debbi and I could remember. To top it off, we received the trophy for the best (only) vehicle in the show, hand made by one of the residents.

We know we are told to not lean on our own understanding, but Debbi and I were both feeling like my health and strength were improving to a point where the Holy Spirit might be giving us glimpses of our next direction. I was now cancer free. My bone marrow transplant last December was successful. There is no such thing as an instant recovery, however. Even with a 100% donor match, there are issues, especially with someone my age.

My immune system had to be "trained" to recognize my different organs and play nice. So far, I had had GVHD in my digestive system, mouth, and eyes. Targeted chemotherapy was used in each case to combat the GVHD. The BK virus attacks people with compromised immune systems, especially transplant patients and it often moves from organ to organ. I had to battle the BK virus in my urinary system and in my kidneys. It would likely never be eliminated, but it was now under control.

I had lost 50 pounds, mostly muscle. I was very weak and fatigued easily. I was going to PT twice a week in Dallas and doing exercises at home every other day. My blood work improved gradually, and as my RBC and oxygen transfer improved. My critical blood components continued to improve, but until all of them were in the "normal" ranges, I remained very susceptible to infection. Viruses, fungal infections, common germs, cuts and scrapes could all put me back in the ICU in short order.

I say this to let you know that while you may want so badly to return to "normal", you still must be careful. If your friends are not sick and haven't been around anyone who has been sick, tell them they can shake your hand and hug your neck. But tell them to not get their feelings hurt if you back away from them if they cough or sneeze, or if you wear a mask. We regularly thanked our friends and relatives for their understanding and prayers. God had been so good to us during this journey.

> "Fear not, for I am with you; be not dismayed, for I am your God. I will strengthen you, Yes, I will help you, I will hold you with My righteous right hand." Isaiah 41:10, NKJV

On June 21, six months almost to the day, I received a call from outpatient surgery at the hospital to schedule the removal of my Tri-fusion port. I would continue to have blood work done on a regular basis and infusions in the future, but no longer large scale. Debbi and I were elated and thanked God in heaven, our Stonewater family, our friends and neighbors and kids and grandkids who had prayed for us and encouraged us. The port was removed June 25th. Normally a routine procedure that only requires local anesthesia, mine was nothing but. The surgeon remarked that my body had "claimed" the port and was not giving it up easily. The normal 10-minute surgery turned into a 45-minute ordeal. Note to self: Don't assume anything.

The following Tuesday was another day of good news and not so good news. My blood work had gone south again. My care team drew additional blood samples and did more tests to determine what the problem was. My oncologist suspected another virus. She increased the dosage on some of my medications, and said we would be continuing weekly visits until she got it figured out. My kidney and liver functions were very good, praise God.

The following Monday, my PT session went well, but their focus was still on my upper body. They were backed up with appointments and short on personnel who do lower body PT, so my doctor approved moving my PT to a facility in Granbury. I reported to the lab at

9:45am Tuesday morning and had blood drawn through a regular IV in my arm; the first one in a long time. We met with my case manager afterwards and discussed the lab analysis, which showed improvement, but still way low in some categories. Medications were adjusted, and their mood remained optimistic. The plan was lab analysis every two weeks and my doctor approved of us moving out of the hotel. Quoting our friend Tom Cunningham, "God was on the move."

My lab results a week later included 14 "flags". The most alarming was creatinine level, which was almost double the previous week's reading and indicated a kidney function problem. Not good. More blood and a urine sample were taken. Both were sent to the lab. I went to the hospital infusion floor and received a liter of fluids to hydrate my kidneys through a third IV. I missed my Tri-fusion ports. My lab results three days later showed some improvement. The medication changes and the IV fluids addressed the kidney malfunction, and results were back to normal. My WBC and RBC were going up as well. Praise God.

My lab results were very encouraging Monday morning, July 16. There were only six "flags" compared to 14 a week ago. My WBC, hemoglobin, and platelets had increased. My kidney and liver functions remained normal, but I got an infusion of fluids to help with electrolyte imbalance. I started physical therapy in Granbury Tuesday morning to begin working on leg strengthening.

If you find yourself in a situation like mine, where you have regular (and irregular) doctor visits, infusions, physical therapy sessions, trips to the pharmacy, and other activities related to your illness, you may find yourself in an environment where most of your time, efforts, and thoughts are on your illness. I encourage you to find a way to step out of that environment when possible. It is too easy to get discouraged or even depressed. Look around you and see how so many others are less fortunate. Some people have no insurance. Some people have lost their home. Some people have little or no family support. Count your blessings. Remember things you like to do. Debbi and I played Scrabble often, a game we had always enjoyed together. Be with friends, when possible. Get out of the house if you can. Go to church or watch church services online. Don't disconnect from others, and most importantly, don't disconnect from God. Pray often. God is always listening.

Debbi and I booked a cabin near Fredericksburg, TX where we had planned to spend a few days in rocking chairs on the porch relaxing. We left after my PT session and were about an hour out of town when our neighbors Kevin and Robbie, who take care of our dogs, called and told us they both had COVID. We all agreed it would be best if they didn't go into our home, and they should concentrate on taking care of themselves! Barry, one of our other neighbors, agreed to pinch hit and care for our dogs. We thanked Barry profusely and prayed for Kevin and Robbie.

When we got to the cabin near Fredericksburg, we were disappointed to find both rocking chairs were broken, there were pieces of glass in the front door where the windows had been poorly replaced, and there was no closet. I immediately called the VRBO rental agent, was told there were no other cabins available, and our payment was not refundable. I called the credit card company, requested they reverse the charges, and we moved to a hotel in town – not what we had planned for a getaway. While in Fredericksburg, we were able to visit our dear friend Bob. The trip was a nice departure from what had become our new routine.

I got good reports from the lab and doctor in Dallas the next Monday. Four of my medication dosages were being reduced! My WBC increased 20% during the past week, and my platelets level was so good I was going back on my Eliquis. We were going to Dallas just once per week now, God willing. I was so grateful for my cheerleader wife, friends, family, and prayer warriors.

The following Monday, the lab reports were not so good. My WBC went down from 4.0 to 3.1 (normal range is 4.8 to 10.8), my RBC went down from 3.01 to 2.72 (normal range is 4.7 to 6.1), and my platelets took a dive from 96 to 73 (normal range is 130 to 400). My doctor suspected another virus, so more blood was drawn for additional analysis. My kidney and liver functions were both good. I got an infusion of fluids for hydration and a blood infusion. I would go back in four days for follow up – so much for once a week visits. While this back and forth was frustrating, I was still grateful I was still in the race.

We told ourselves we would look back on this someday and say, "So that's what God was up to ... now it makes sense."

My oncologist called the next day and confirmed the additional lab tests revealed I had a new virus that my immune system was trying to fight. They called in a prescription to a pharmacy in Granbury so I could begin taking it immediately and wanted me back in Dallas in three days for follow up lab tests. Debbi and I met with my oncologist Friday morning and the lab work showed things going back in the right direction. She adjusted some of my other medication dosages, and said I would not need any infusions that day. Thank you, Jesus! We had discovered the virus and reacted quickly. My oncologist was confident the new anti-virus medication would help my immune system keep it under control. On the way back to Granbury, we stopped for lunch at The Rim restaurant in Fort Worth and celebrated. It was very nice sitting in a restaurant booth instead of an infusion chair.

On August 9 Debbi and I met with my oncologist after lab work and got more news that indicated I might be out of the woods soon. Of the ten blood components "flagged" lower than normal last Friday, all ten had improved that week. Some were approaching normal ranges, and some had quite a way to go, but all were going in the right direction. The next Tuesday, my lab reports were good again, with no big changes. Both viruses I had were now under control. Dosages on two of my anti-viral medications and one of my immunosuppressants were being reduced further.

Two weeks prior, I could not kneel onto my knees and get back up without assistance. On this day, I could. I decided this was an exercise I would add to my home PT routine. I was going to get down on my knees and thank God every day for never leaving me through these challenges and giving me more strength every day.

On August 21 all my lab results were either the same or slightly better. My liver and kidney functions were good, and there was no need for any infusions. My oncologist reduced the dosage on some more of my medications, and I didn't have to go back for eight days. We were optimistic, and I was feeling better every day. I was still very weak, but physical therapy twice a week was helping. My immune system was still about half normal. Debbi and I reminded ourselves that it is futile to try and predict when my treatments would be over, and I would be well – only God knows.

"But I will hope continually, And will praise You yet more and more." Psalms 71:14, NKJV

Conclusion

As of this writing, my immune system is gradually getting stronger. I am still going to Dallas for lab work and doctor visits every two weeks. Our lives are on the path back to normal. I keep listening to my body, reporting symptoms to my doctor, doing my physical therapy home exercises, and being cautious about exposure to people who might be sick with anything contagious. Next week, we will celebrate one year since my transplant.

GVHD keeps tormenting me. Over the past several months, I've developed several skin carcinomas that required four surgeries to remove them. These were caused by exposure to the sun, a condition I now had to be especially aware of because one of my medications increased my risk fifty-fold. A couple of weeks ago, I got a rash on my back and chest that was like hundreds of ant bites. Steroids and other medication changes got rid of the rash. The steroids had their own side effects, which were not pleasant, but went away once I no longer had to take them. Now a new virus has become very active in my system, and I may have to undergo weekly infusions to combat it.

"There was a study a few years ago, and I think they surveyed over 2,000 people, the majority of whom, 70%, said that their faith had gotten stronger as a result of their diagnosis" said Dr. John Peeteet, a psychiatrist at Brigham and Women's Hospital and Dana-Faber Cancer Institute in Boston. Cure magazine, Summer 2024 edition.

My faith has gotten stronger because of my cancer. I immediately leaned on God and asked Him to take control. The following two years were a roller coaster of testing, waiting, treatments, setbacks, and accomplishments. Yes, I experienced pain and suffering. I prayed every day, often several times a day. God answered my prayers. Reading my Bible every day was a huge inspiration.

The Bible says we can experience joy in suffering. What!? The first time I heard that, I thought "Those two words don't belong in the same sentence." Look at these two scriptures:

> "These things I have spoken to you, that in Me you may have peace. In the world you will have tribulation; but be of good cheer, I have overcome the world." John 16:33, NKJV

> "My brethren, count it all joy when you fall into various trials, knowing that the testing of your faith produces patience." James 1:2-3, NKJV

Jesus told us we would have troubles. Even though we believe in Him, we are still human, and we live in this broken world. But as believers and followers of Jesus, we can have JOY in knowing that SUFFERING is of this world, and we have everlasting life waiting on us, where there is no suffering for eternity.

So how did cancer and the testing of my faith produce strength? God uses our trials to sharpen us and draw us closer to Him. I had a lot of time to read my Bible and study for my seminary classes. I was given many opportunities to share my faith with others. Some days, I barely had the energy to put one foot in front of the other. But I reminded myself to not look down at my feet. Instead, I looked up, down the hallways and sidewalks, and focused on the future and God's promise of everlasting life.

I hope my story will encourage you to lean on your faith and God if you find yourself in a situation where you are faced with a life-threatening illness. Don't give up. Don't be a quitter. I truly believe my illness has been a test to see if I would stay focused on God, and not on me. I am alive today because I gave up control and trusted Him. I give God all the credit, all the glory.

If you are not sure about your faith, I hope you will ask Jesus into your heart. Find yourself a church to attend. Start attending online if you are confined to a hospital. Find yourself some friends you can talk to about faith. Read and study your Bible. Get a Bible if you don't have one. And pray. God is always listening.

Acknowledgements

I want to thank God for saving my life here on Earth. The trials and suffering have strengthened my faith in ways I never would have accomplished on my own. This book never would have been written if I hadn't had the opportunities to share my faith through this illness journey. I truly believe He is not done with me yet.

To Stonewater Church, the IMPACT group, and the Thursday morning Men's Study Group, thank you for praying for us and providing support and encouragement. Thank you for being our church family. Thank you for encouraging me to put my testimony in writing to share with others.

To my family and friends, thank you for encouraging me to send the daily updates, constantly checking on me, and listening to all my stories. A special thank you to those who reviewed my draft manuscript and offered feedback.

To Tricia Bullard, thank you for sharing your testimony in your own book, "Road To Bethel" and encouraging me to write a book to share my faith. You have been an inspiration.

Finally, I want to express my love for my wife, Debbi. She reminded me more than once that we were in this together. She suffered right along with me. Our marriage has been strengthened and our love for each other has increased. Debbi encouraged me to put my story into words, putting up with countless hours I spent in my study, listening to my ideas, and helping with proofreading and feedback during the whole writing process.

About the Author

Bill Greenwade was born in McAllen, Texas and went to school from second grade to graduation from high school in the small town of Refugio, Texas. He graduated from Texas A&M University in 1975. He has lived in several cities in Texas, Arkansas, Pennsylvania, and Georgia and his career allowed him to travel to many countries. For several years, Bill lived in his motorhome and traveled across the United States volunteering at National and State Parks. He is 71 years old and lives in Granbury, Texas with his wife Debbi. They have a blended family of five children and four grandchildren. He is a member of Stonewater Church in Granbury. Bill is involved in church groups including the IMPACT empty nesters group, a Thursday morning

Men's Sermon-Based Bible study group and a Faith and Healing group. He has completed the first year of a two-year seminary program. Bill's hobbies include motorcycling and travel. He enjoys walks with the family dogs, fly-fishing, jigsaw puzzles, baking cookies, and grilling on his patio smoker.

Printed in the United States
by Baker & Taylor Publisher Services